CONTENTS

Breeds

Beautiful CATS

The Most Popular Breeds

Uschi Birr

Sterling Publishing Co., Inc.
New York

Photo Credits

Angermayer/Reinhard: 10, 16, 48 below, 51 left, 57 top right, 80, 84, 90 below left;
Bernie: 6;
Horst Bielfeld: 69 below;
Cogies: 20;
Excalibur: 8 top right, 19 top right, 26 below left, 41 top, 51 right, 55 top, 57 below, 63 below, 64 center, 73 top, 73 below, 74 top, 74 center, 88, 89 top, 90 top, 92, 93 top right, 93 below;
Français: 23 top right, 29 top right, 29 below;
Gengoux: 32;
Hannelore Grimm: 44 below, 77 below;
Hermeline: 45 top;
Herz für Tiere: (Archive: 62; Mike Moritz: 25 below; Gerd Pfeiffer: 77 top; Ulrike Schanz: 4, 8 below, 12 below, 13 below, 14, 15, 29 top left, 30 top, 52 top, 52 top left; Karin Skogstad: 11 below, 12 top right, 13 top, 70 below, 71, 83);
Juniors Picture Archive: (Kolmikov: 47 below; Liebold: 43 top, 87; Schanz: 12 top, 17, 27 below, 67 top, 67 center);

Labat: 7 left, 9 top, 18, 19 top left, 19 below, 21, 23 below, 25 top, 26 top, 26 top right, 33, 34 left, 34 right, 36 top, 39 below, 44 top left, 54 top, 54 below, 55 below right, 56, 57 left, 61 top left, 64 below, 65, 66 left, 66 center, 75 top, 75 below, 78 top, 85 top, 86 top right, 86 top right, 91, 95 top left;
Labat/Lanceau: 52 top right, 52 below;
Lanceau: 20, 22 top, 22 below, 23 top left, 24, 27 top, 27 below, 30 below, 31 top, 31 below, 35 below, 38, 39 center, 40 left, 40 right, 41 center, 49, 58 top, 58 below, 59, 60 top, 60 center, 61 top right, 62, 63 top, 64 top left, 64 top right, 66 below, 67 below, 72, 76, 78 below, 85 below, 86 top left, 86 below, 90 below right, 93 top left, 94 top, 94 top, 94 below;
Lili: 7 right;
Lothar Lenz: 5;
Werner Layer: 44 top right, 68, 69 top

Library of Congress Cataloging-in-Publication Data

Birr, Uschi.
  Beautiful cats : the most popular breeds / by Uschi Birr.
    p. cm.
  Includes index.
  ISBN 0-8069-9993-4
  1. Cat breeds, I. Title.
SF442.B5813 1998
636.8—dc21

97-50631
CIP

Translated by Elisabeth Reinersmann
Edited by Rodman Neumann

1 3 5 7 9 10 8 6 4 2

Published 1998 by Sterling Publishing Company, Inc.
387 Park Avenue South, New York, N.Y. 10016
Originally published and © 1996, Franckh-Kosmos Verlag-GmbH & Co., Stuttgart
in German as part of *Mit Katzen leben*
English translation © 1998 by Sterling Publishing Co., Inc.
Distributed in Canada by Sterling Publishing
℅ Canadian Manda Group, One Atlantic Avenue, Suite 105
Toronto, Ontario, Canada M6K 3E7
Distributed in Great Britain and Europe by Cassell PLC
Wellington House, 125 Strand, London WC2R 0BB, England
Distributed in Australia by Capricorn Link (Australia) Pty Ltd.
P.O. Box 6651, Baulkham Hills, Business Centre, NSW 2153, Australia
Printed in Hong Kong
All rights reserved

Sterling ISBN 0-8069-9993-4

What Is a Recognized Breed?

Everybody knows that domestic cats come in many different sizes, shapes, colors, and body structures. Whenever a certain characteristic (for instance, long hair, markings, size) is handed down to the next generation, a breed has developed within the family of cats. Two cat fancy associations—TICA (The International Cat Association) and the CFA (Cat Fanciers' Association)—decide if special characteristics are sufficient to consider its carrier as part of a separate breed. The largest organization in Europe is TICA, represented in every country and to which local organizations belong. The CFA is primarily represented in Asia and the United States, but also has representatives in Europe.

Both organizations attempt to cooperate with each other in order to eliminate possible confusion about breeds and their particular characteristics.

This book deals primarily with breeds recognized by TICA.

STANDARDS

For each breed, standards have been established that describe what should be the ideal appearance (or type) of the breed as well as features such as coloration and patterning.

Standards play a great role in any exhibition or competition because the jury, presented with different members of a certain breed, must decide which of the animals adheres closest to the standards laid down on paper. The cat that adheres closest to an established standard is then awarded first place. Other entries may be given ribbons with acclamations such as excellent, very good, or good.

ASSOCIATIONS

Pedigrees need to be assigned, new breeds need to be critically examined, exhibitions must be organized, and champions must be created. Many a cat fancier association owes its existence to these necessities.

But associations and clubs do more: their members are informed about developments in care, upkeep, feeding, and breeding as well as health regulations such as the prohibition against breeding defective animals that may imperil the standards for a particular breed.

Each principal organization has regional groups in many cities that not only cater to local breeders but also create adoption facilities for young animals as well as information centers.

Above: The Tonkinese, a Siamese-Burmese cross with a more rounded body than Siamese, is recognized in both the United States and Canada but not in England, where Siamese and Burmese are not as different as they are in North America.

Left page: A standard determines the ideal condition and color of the coat, the physique, and eye color.

Siamese

An Elf full of Passion

They move with refined grace and charm. The wisdom of the Far East emanates from their bright, ocean-blue eyes. However, oriental gentleness is foreign to the Siamese. Her life is one of burning passion, stormy temperament, and never-ending energy. She is very affectionate and demanding, but never boring.

ORIGIN

The deep respect Buddhists have towards animals, and specifically to those with light or white coloring, was probably the reason that made the existence of this oldest of all cat breeds possible. It would have been impossible to create this breed if people had not isolated the first Siamese cats, preventing crossbreeding with cats of different colors. Only when Siamese cats are paired among themselves does the typical mask and pointed look remain intact.

The history of the Siamese cat most likely began in the 14th century. A picture dating back to 1350 —now in the National Library in Bangkok—shows a cat with light fur, but also with dark feet, tail, and face (pointed). In 1793 the German explorer and natural scientist Peter Simon Pallas made a sketch of a cat that he had seen on his travels to the Caspian Sea. It showed the characteristic markings of a Siamese cat: a long, thin tail, a body more elegant than cats of that day, and an extremely lively temperament. The face was rounder than those of today.

Siamese cats were brought to Europe by English travelers at the end of the 19th century, perhaps gifts of the King of Siam. They were such a sensation at the Cat Exhibition at the Crystal Palace in London that a literal import fever was set in motion.

"Siamese fever" spread from England to the European continent and the United States, but Siamese cats were rare and expensive. Even after World War I, one of these blue-eyed beauties could only be bought at a price that was the equivalent of precious jewels. Their popularity led to the introduction of new breeds. As these appeared, the Siamese became only one of many Orientals. The popularity of the Siamese decreased at least until the 1930s, when in addition to the traditional seal points other colors appeared, including blue- and chocolate-colored markings. These new colors prompted TICA to set new stan-

Above: The Siamese tabby point with its striped markings is recognized in the United States as an Oriental Shorthair.

Left column: Young cats already show the points; here, a tabby not yet fully developed.

Left page: Seal-point Siamese, the most common color variation. With increasing age the light undercoat becomes darker.

TIPS FOR CARE

Rub down with a suede cloth and the short coat will take on a silky sheen.

Above right: Siamese red point.

Below, center and right: Blue-tortie-point and seal-tortie-point Siamese.

Below left: The Foreign White, known internationally as the Oriental White. The White is indistinguishable from her Siamese ancestors in all but fur coloration, but is now considered one of the Oriental Shorthair breeds.

dards which gave modern Siamese breeds their physique and multitude of colors. As the shape of the head became more wedge-like, Siamese appeared in many more different color varieties. With the build more slender, the coat lighter, and the blue eyes more intense, their character did not change, however.

CHARACTER AND TEMPERAMENT

Siamese are very comfortable among their own. And even though they also are friendly towards dogs, what they love most of all are people. Their need for human contact makes them a constant companion, no matter where

we go. They love to put their front legs around their person's shoulder and neck, and they most certainly love to roll up in any lap that is available.

Siamese hate to be alone—and to avoid this they will pursue their owner with cunning, intelligence, and intensity. No doorknob is safe, no wall thick enough to ignore their penetrating call for people. The voice is anything but elf-like; it is loud, melodious, and has a tremendous range. Siamese can mew, chirp, sing, warble, yodel, wine, lure, snarl, and, of course, purr. They love to chatter and will answer with a song when they hear their name.

Your Siamese is very trainable. She will "heel" without a command, she will come when called and retrieve when asked. Siamese will roll over and jump as you desire. Play is part of their life; it is their form of exercise that allows them to give free rein to their temperament.

But this thoroughbred also has a gentle side: she senses conflict in the family, she knows when a member is sick or is crying, and promptly turns into a "super mom"—she will give comfort and reassurance, she distracts and cuddles, she shows soul and sympathy, she is cheerful and will bring a laugh to her companion, no matter how he feels.

A Siamese cat loses nothing of her charm and fire as she ages. She becomes wiser—but never quieter. In spite of her delicate body the Siamese is among those breeds that live the longest. Twenty years or more is not uncommon.

TYPE AND STANDARD

TYPE, BODY, LEGS, TAIL

This cat is slim, elegant, medium in size, agile, and muscular. The body is long and slim, the shoulders are not wider than the hips. Legs are long and have small, oval paws. The tail is very long and thin, tapering to a fine point.

HEAD AND EARS

The medium-sized head is wedge shaped with straight lines, a long straight nose, and a flat forehead without a break. The ears are pointed, large, wide at the base.

EYES

Eyes are of medium size, almond shaped, and slightly angled. They are clear, transparent, bright, and the color is a deep blue.

COAT

The coat is very short, fine, glossy, silky, and close to the body.

COLORS

The body color should be even and clearly in contrast with the pointed markings. The mask of the face, the markings on the ears, legs, and tail should be the same shade.

Seal point, blue point, chocolate point, and lilac point are recognized in the United States. Additional colors (included in the Colorpoint and Oriental Shorthairs in the U.S.) are red point, cream point, seal-tortie point, blue-tortie point, chocolate-tortie point, lilac-tortie point, seal-tabby point, blue-tabby point, chocolate-tabby point, lilac-tabby point, red-tabby point, cream-tabby point, seal-torbie point, blue-torbie point, chocolate-torbie point, and lilac-torbie point. Tortie point is dabbled with red or cream, with clearly defined spots. Tabby point mask shows stripes on the cheeks and spots on the whisker pads. Ears have a thumb print on the back, the legs show stripes, and the back paw pads are uniform in color. The tail has regular stripes with a unicolored tip.

Top:Seal point, the traditional color of the Siamese: the points are a deep, dark seal-brown.

Seal tabby point, with a distinct M-shape on its forehead.

NOTE ON COLOR NAMES

Tortie is simply an abbreviation for Tortoiseshell.

Torties are usually female, showing black and light and dark red areas in the coat. Tortie and White is commonly known in North America as Calico.

Torbie is a Tortoiseshell Tabby.

Oriental Shorthair

Oriental Shorthair: Grace Full of Elegance

Their movements are graceful and smooth, their voice is powerful and demanding. They rule their empire with an iron will—in spite of their delicate stature. When intelligence and physical strength won't get them what they want, they will use their charm.

ORIGIN

Their first appearance in Europe was unspectacular. Together with ivory-colored Siamese beauties that sported ebony markings and sky-blue eyes, there also came in 1814 from Bangkok a hazelnut-brown cat with emerald-green eyes; and she immediately disappeared into private hands. Siamese cats of a different kind (imported later) also found very little favor.

Europe was overcome by a Siamese fever. They found little that was appealing about these brown, green-eyed cats—not until the beginning of the twentieth century when the English discovered that by pairing house cats with Siamese they

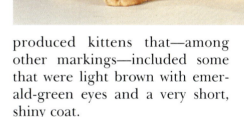

produced kittens that—among other markings—included some that were light brown with emerald-green eyes and a very short, shiny coat.

A few Siamese cat breeders very deliberately continued such pairings, and one of them brought forth "Elmtower Susannah," a cat of a gently colored chestnut brown. Her coat color made history when it was renamed as the Havana.

As with all Oriental cat breeds with differently colored coats—to date there are more than fifty—they were, at first, thought of separate-

Above: Spotted-tabby Oriental Shorthair. The spots and markings have to be distinctly separate from the lighter coat.

Left: The large ears and slanted eyes give these felines a look of wonder.

Left page: Chocolate-tabby Oriental Shorthair. The markings in young animals are not yet clearly defined.

NOTE

The term Oriental describes a cat of fine-boned, svelte, "foreign" appearance.

ly and given their own names. The diluted variety of the Havana, a pinkish blue-coated cat, was called "Oriental Lavender," and the ebony-black type was given the name "Ebony Oriental." Scarcely had the breeders discovered they could produce many colors and markings, than the breeding of the Oriental Shorthairs experienced a tremendous upsurge.

CHARACTER AND TEMPERAMENT

Intensity, persistence, and passionate affection are the characteristics of the Oriental Shorthair. Patience, laissez-faire, or giving in is not part of their repertoire. They do what they do with un-

Above: Lavender is the term for these lilac Oriental Shorthairs.

Above right: A slender body, small agile neck, large ears, and a long, thin whip-like tail contribute to the sleekness of the breed.

Right: Ebony is the name given to the black Oriental Shorthair.

swerving intensity and—like the Siamese—they are also devoted and bond easily. This affection is already evident to the breeder, whom they will greet and follow, recognizing him by footsteps and voice alone, when they are not quite three weeks old.

Families that have decided to bring an Oriental Shorthair into the house will also find this out quickly. Those who leave in the morning are escorted to the door and greeted when they come home. A bed is never off-limits because this slender cat—without fail—will have already claimed it as her own. Oriental Shorthairs will even overcome their aversion to water just to be there when you take a shower or bath; they will disregard their normal need for sleep when a human being is calling; and they will cuddle with people even more than they need to be cuddled themselves.

What they also have in common with the Siamese is the voice and their ability to express themselves melodically: when body language and soulful eyes don't work, the Oriental Shorthair will use her voice to get attention.

TYPE AND STANDARD

TYPE, BODY, LEGS, TAIL

This cat is slender and muscular with long lines; it has a long, slender neck and shoulders that are not wider than the hips. The legs are long and delicate with small, oval paws. The very long, thin tail is narrow at the base, tapering to a fine tip.

HEAD, EARS, EYES

A wedge-shaped head with a long, straight nose, small mouth, and medium-sized jaw. Ears are large, wide at the base, and pointed. Medium-sized eyes are almond shaped, slightly slanted, and preferably a brilliant, lively green.

COAT

Very short, fine, glossy, and silky; close to the body.

COLORS

Solid or bicolored animals have an evenly colored coat without shading or tabby markings. Whiskers and eyebrows harmonize with the body color.

RECOGNIZED COLOR VARIETIES

Solid: ebony, blue, chocolate, lavender, red, cream, cinnamon, and fawn (beige).

Tortoiseshell: black, blue-chocolate, lavender, cinnamon, and fawn.

Smoke: black, blue, chocolate, lavender, red, cream, cinnamon, fawn, tortie, blue tortie, chocolate tortie, lilac tortie, cinnamon tortie, and fawn tortie.

Tabby: black, blue-chocolate, lilac, red, cream, cinnamon, fawn, black tortie, blue tortie, chocolate tortie, lavender tortie, cinnamon tortie, and fawn tortie.

Silver tabby: black, blue-chocolate, lavender, red, cream, cinnamon, fawn, black tortie, blue tortie, chocolate tortie, lavender tortie, cinnamon tortie, and fawn tortie.

TIPS FOR CARE

The slender body is deceiving: Oriental Shorthairs are no lightweights or meager eaters. They need the same nutrition as any other cat, sometimes even more because they use a lot of energy when playing.

Left: Temperament and body structure of Oriental Shorthairs are very similar to those of their Siamese cousins.

Javanese

Exotic Creatures from 1001 Nights

Oriental bloodline with silky, long hair may sound odd, but in reality it isn't. Delicately limbed with bat-like ears like their short-haired relatives, Javanese are just as clever and sure of themselves. Each is a bundle of dynamite wrapped in a veil of silky hair.

ORIGIN

There is still a great deal of confusion over the name Javanese. In the 1940s long-haired kittens appeared in Siamese litters in the United States. Breeders had little interest, fearing they would be suspected of out-crossing.

As these kittens became known, their popularity spread. It proved quite difficult to know what to call them. Different clubs and organizations adopted a confusion of names: Siamese Longhair, Balinese, Javanese, Mandarin, Oriental Longhair, and Somali. Fanciers objected to the use of the name "Siamese" for these natural variants, so they became widely known as Balinese.

However, in the United States the CFA recognized only the four traditional colors of Siamese as Balinese in 1963, all others generally being known as Javanese. It was much later, in 1987, that the CFA formally accepted the Javanese, still considering them to

be variant "Balinese" that are other than the traditional Siamese colors. To add further confusion, in New Zealand self and spotted forms of the Balinese are called Javanese, while in Britain all long-haired variants of Siamese are known as Balinese, and the name

Left: The coat of a kitten is still short, not growing to its final length until about six months.

Below: Head and ears are small, long, and delicate; the same as Oriental Shorthairs. Only the length of the hair distinguishes the two breeds.

Javanese is there reserved for cats that emerged from a breeding program to recreate the old Turkish Angora. The British Angora was recognized in 1984, and named Javanese in 1989 to match its Oriental appearance.

CHARACTER AND TEMPERAMENT

Everything about the Javanese cat is graceful and elegant. Light footed and effortless is their acro-

batic dance, rubbing against a person's leg with sensitive tact.

They love to play but are not noisy. they will conquer every surface in the house without destroying anything in the process. They can satisfy their hunting instinct with crumpled paper or a toy mouse. No movement in their environment escapes their emerald-green eyes.

Blue and blue-tabby Javanese.

TYPE AND STANDARD

TYPE, BODY, LEGS, TAIL

A slender, well-muscled cat with tapered lines, a long narrow neck, and a slender, long body. The legs are delicate and long, the paws small and oval. The comparably long, thin tail is narrow at the base and tapers to a fine tip.

HEAD, EARS, EYES

The medium-sized head is wedge shaped with straight lines and a long, straight nose. The ears are big, well pointed, and broad at the base. The eyes are of medium size, almond shaped, and slightly angled; their color is a vibrant, brilliant green-blue.

COAT

Fine and silky, medium long around the body, somewhat longer around the neck, shoulder and tail, which spreads to form a plume. No dense undercoat.

COLORS

One-, two-, or three-colored cats are uniform in color without tabby markings. The whiskers and eyebrows harmonize with the color of the body.

Black, blue, chocolate, lilac, red, cream, cinnamon, and fawn.

Tortoiseshell: black, blue, chocolate, lilac, cinnamon, and fawn.

Smoke: black, blue, chocolate, lilac, red, cream, cinnamon, fawn, black tortie, blue tortie, chocolate tortie, lilac tortie, cinnamon tortie, and fawn tortie.

Tabby: black, blue, chocolate, lilac, red, cream, cinnamon, fawn, black tortie, blue tortie, chocolate tortie, lilac tortie, cinnamon tortie, and fawn tortie.

Silver tabby: black, blue, chocolate, lilac, red, cream, cinnamon, fawn, black tortie, blue tortie, chocolate tortie, lilac tortie, cinnamon tortie, and fawn tortie.

Balinese

Masked Beauty
with an Ermine Coat

Previous page: In England all long-haired Orientals with any conceivable color combination or markings of the Siamese, Colorpoint Shorthairs, or Oriental Shorthairs are known as Balinese (here: seal-tabby point).

Below: Long, blue, flowing hair covers the tail because the undercoat is missing: Balinese blue point.

A cat of contrasts—the svelte body is wrapped in a flowing, delicate, silky coat with dark accents without the extra bulk of an undercoat. As is the appearance, so is the Balinese's temperament: full of gentle charm and then suddenly an exuberant little devil.

ORIGIN

People still argue about how the gene for long hair was introduced into a breed with such short hair as that of the Siamese. Whether it was a long-ago pairing between a Persian and a Siamese or the result of random mutation, the first long-haired Siamese appeared early in the twentieth century, but were given away without a pedigree. As mentioned for the Javanese, the reason was that Siamese cat breeders had little interest in a cat that might lead to rumors that they had introduced other breeds. By the 1950s, after long-haired, pure-bred Siamese

They are persistent in getting their way. They will give love in abundance—but only if they want to. Curiosity is paired with caution—which bodes well for furnishings and knickknacks.

continued to appear over and over, fanciers in the United States had become fond of them and began to develop the breed. But it was not until 1963 that the CFA recognized the Balinese—restricted to long-haired animals that displayed only the four traditional Siamese colors. In 1983 TICA also recognized Balinese as a breed. In Britain, and as shown here, all color variants of long-haired Orientals are lumped together as Balinese.

CHARACTER AND TEMPERAMENT

A cat that hides its sensibilities. If insulted, she will not scratch but withdraw. She does not express her joys exuberantly, but would rather curl up in somebody's lap and purr blissfully. She can watch for hours on end on a windowsill only to suddenly explode—leaping through the house. She may stop in the middle of joyful play, or after a session of grooming, and disappear under the couch.

TYPE AND STANDARD

TYPE, BODY, LEGS, TAIL

The ideal Balinese cat is svelte, but still muscular. Neck and body are long and slender, but the shoulders not wider than hips. The long legs have small oval paws. The very long, thin tail tapers to a fine tip.

HEAD, EARS, EYES

The head is of medium size and wedge shaped with straight lines. The long, straight nose extends to the forehead without a break. The mouth is small; the large, pointed ears are wide at the base. The almond-shaped eyes are slightly slanted and of clear, deep, vivid blue.

COAT

The coat is fine and silky, medium long; somewhat longer at the shoulder and neck, but without a mane. Tail is plumed like a feather duster. A furry undercoat is absent.

COLORS

The color of the marking in the face, ears, legs and tail should be as uniform as possible. The color of the coat around the body should also be uniformly even and be in clear contrast to the markings.

RECOGNIZED COLOR VARIATIONS

The four main colorpoints are seal point, blue point, chocolate point, and lilac point. Other colors include red point, cream point, seal-tortie point, blue-tortie point, chocolate-tortie point, and lilac-tortie point. Tabby point: seal, blue, chocolate, lilac, red, cream, seal tortie, blue tortie, chocolate tortie, and lilac tortie.

Above: During the winter Balinese cats will grow a long ruff around the neck (chocolate point).

Upper left: A silky-haired, slender beauty: a graceful Balinese (chocolate tabby).

Russian Blue

Blue Angel with a Silvery Sheen

There is a hint of melancholy in the expression of her eyes. The coat is the color of the Polar Sea. Her character is shaped by gentleness and dignity. Flamboyant entrances she leaves to others. She appears silently on the scene and opens her soul only to those she is in tune with.

ORIGIN

English merchant mariners established a trading center in 1553 at the White Sea, which 60 years later was called Archangelsk. They used it as an intermediary anchoring place and shelter when traveling in the region that was covered with ice floes almost 200 days out of the year. One of the mariners who landed must have seen one of these blue kittens and petted it. Otherwise they may never have been known in Europe.

These harbor cats—living wild in Archangelsk—have something very special: a double coat—like an ice bear—that repels water and protects against cold. The sailors were fascinated by this and in 1860 brought these faintly blue cats with their bright green eyes to England, where they were met with disappointment. In vogue were the Chartreux, who had an intense blue coat, emerald-green eyes, and a robust body.

For more than 100 years the delicate Russian cat remained in the shadow of its splendid rival. It was bred to either become a Siamese look-alike or to conform to the powerful British look, and in the process lost more and more of

Above: When observed in light, the coat of the Russian Blue shows its characteristic silver glow.

Left page: The fur is dense and silky to the touch, double and plush athough quite short.

Above: Eyes shine in bright green.

Below: The short, fine, and very dense coat, a so-called double coat, distinguishes the Russian Blue from other blue cats.

its unique characteristics, until English breeders, remembering the original Archangelsk cat, began to develop a standard that would reestablish its traditional appearance.

CHARACTER AND TEMPERAMENT

This little blue angel cannot hide its Russian soul. At first quietly reserved, this cat will divide her environment into that which is acceptable and worthy of her devotion and that which is to be avoided. She takes time making her decisions, but, once made, it may never change.

She will approach those she loves with self-confidence and pride. Her person is allowed to stroke her but cannot force her to do anything. She enjoys curling up in a lap and talking philosophy with half-opened eyes and an unfathomable expression.

pushy. She has a robust constitution that loves—even in cold or rainy weather—to be outside, where she lets the world pass by and where she is always ready for a short hunt.

Strangers are approached with caution and mistrust. Force of any kind she hates—just as much as she does noise and commotion. She is almost always the traditional one-person cat that will only give unconditional devotion to the one to whom she becomes a quiet, gentle, and absolutely faithful companion.

She is always ready to participate in any games, provided nobody makes fun of her or plays tricks. The Russian Blue is very fair; there is not a nasty streak in her, she is always direct, but never

TYPE AND STANDARD

TYPE, BODY, LEG AND TAIL

A graceful body, medium bone structure, long, straight neck, delicate, long legs, and small oval paws. The pads are dark lavender color. The tail is relatively long, begins quite thickly and tapers eventually to a tip.

HEAD, EARS, EYES

The head has the shape of a short wedge, with a strong chin and a prominent whisker base. The nose is straight and blue-gray. The large pointed ears are wide at the base; the skin is thin and translucent, the insides showing a faint covering of fur. The large almond-shaped eyes are wide set and have a bright, lively green color.

COAT

The soft and silky coat is short, dense, very fine, and stands up from the body. The Russian Blue has a double coat.

COLOR

Evenly blue-gray with a distinct silver glow. Black and white forms have been developed in New Zealand and Australia in recent years.

TIPS FOR CARE

The Russian Blue always demands an immaculate, clean toilet box. It is best to make two boxes available—one always being clean.

NOTE

A double coat consists of a thick, longer topcoat over a shorter, soft undercoat. The topcoat comprises guard hairs.

Above left: The Russian Blue is sensitive and will only show affection and devotion after a person has paid enough—and extra—attention to her.

Left: The fur around the nose and paw pads must have the same dark-blue, gray color.

Ocicat

Asphalt Leopard
with a Jungle Look

Breeders have long attempted to cross spotted wild cats with domestic cats to produce the markings and characteristics of their "wild" ancestors. But in spite of its ocelot-like name, the Ocicat has no "wild" ancestors, but got her fiery temperament from her Siamese forefathers and her colors from the Abyssinian.

ORIGIN

Virginia Daly, a breeder living in Michigan, had a plan in the mid-1960s to breed Siamese cats with the agouti points of the Abyssinian. The offsprings again were bred with Siamese and Abyssinian cats. The kittens indeed satisfied the breeder's expectations, except for one kitten which had an ebony-colored fur with golden spots and copper-colored eyes—truly a stranger in the litter. "Tonga," the name of the tomcat, was given away, but throughout the next lit-

ters, golden-spotted kittens appeared until the breeder—a cat lover if there ever was one—abandoned her original plan and dedicated herself to breeding the "Ocicat."

By the late 1960s these spotted cats were already quite popular in the United States, bred in many different colors (the American Shorthair was partially involved in the breeding). The Ocicat was recognized by the CFA in 1987, and in 1990 by TICA.

CHARACTERISTICS AND TEMPERAMENT

Alert but adaptable, sociable but dominant towards other cats, the Ocicat has much in common with

Above: The dark spots on light background develop because each individual hair has bands in different colors. These bands are called ticking. Agouti is the name for this combination of light and dark ticking along the length of individual hairs. Wherever the bands meet, spots will show up in the form of thumb prints.

Left below: The characteristics of an Ocicat are alert ears set slightly at an angle and almond-shaped eyes.

Left page: The first Ocicats exported to Europe from the United States did not yet show the contrast-rich coat.

Center: Cinnamon-spotted Ocicat; the ivory-colored agouti-fur contrasts with cinnamon-colored spots. The ringed tail tapers to a dark tip.

Below left: This chocolate-spotted Ocicat has a warm, ivory-colored base coat with chocolate-colored spots; the light pink nose is outlined in chocolate-brown; the pads are cinnamon colored to chocolate-brown.

Below right: The eyes of Ocicats can be any color other than blue.

her ancestors, without however their exuberant temperament. Of course the Ocicat, too, is very people-oriented but never pushy. She will never refuse to participate in a little game and expects much attention and devotion. But she can also amuse herself with a little ball and initiate a game with people on purpose.

She is receptive towards strangers, monopolizes guests in short order, and shows a good sense of humor with children she accepts as partners. Her size makes for a very robust cat who can put up with quite a bit and yet withdraw in self-defense when there is too much commotion around her.

Many Ocicats learn to walk on a leash or love to ride in a car. She loves to inspect a new environment after her family has moved or remodeled the house. She seems to be interested in any changes, and evaluates them in order to feel quickly at home again. The only thing she hates is being left alone which is likely to bring out a streak of misbehavior. Those who work or otherwise spend a lot of time away from home are well advised to find a partner for their Ocicat.

TIPS FOR CARE

Provide your Ocicat with a stable, high scratching post that gives her a chance for exercise—which she needs a lot of, even inside the house.

TYPE AND STANDARD

TYPE, BODY, LEGS, TAIL

The Ocicat is a medium to large size, well-spotted agouti-cat. She gives the impression of an athletic animal, being very muscular and solidly built, graceful and agile, but with a sturdy build and a full-sized chest. She shows attention to her environment and is very lively. The body is relatively long, powerful, deep, and wide but never ungainly. The bone structure is powerfully developed, muscles are strong, and the chest should be deep with a slight bowing of the rib cage. The back is straight or slightly raised above the back legs, the flanks are straight. The legs are medium long, well shaped, and muscular; the paws are oval and compact. The tail is relatively long, medium thick, and tapers slightly to a usually dark-colored tip.

HEAD, EARS, EYES

The head is moderately wedge-shaped with a slight curve from the mouth to the checks and with a visible but gentle rise from the nose to the eyebrows; the mouth is wide and relatively long, the whisker pad not very well developed. The medium-sized ears are watchful and should have small hair tufts at the tips. The large eyes are almond shaped and set slightly at an angle; every color except blue is allowed.

COAT

The coat is short and sleek, smooth and lustrous with a silky texture. While it is close to the body it is, however, long enough to show the markings. It may not be woolly or long.

COLOR

All colors must be beautiful. The lightest shade of color is usually in the face around the eyes, chin and lower jaw, the darkest at the tip of the tail. Each individual hair, with the exception of the tip of the tail, is banded. Each hair of the markings has a dark tip, while the hair of the base color has light-colored tips. The markings should be distinctive and visible from every direction. The markings of the face, legs, and tail may be darker than those on the body. The base color can be darker on the top than on the underbelly and lighter around the chin and lower jaw.

A broken "necklace" is visible on the throat and lower legs. The round spots are arranged in rows from the shoulder blade, along the spine, and down to the tail. The spots around the shoulders and the hips are randomly arranged and should go down to the legs as far as possible. The side of the body has large, well-distributed thumb-print-shaped spots that are somewhat reminiscent of the classical tabby markings—spots that are surrounded by smaller spots. The tail near the tip shows vertical stripes, ideally alternating with spots.

RECOGNIZED COLOR VARIATIONS

Black (tawny) spotted, blue spotted, chocolate spotted, lavender spotted, cinnamon spotted, fawn spotted.

Silver: black, blue, chocolate, lavender, cinnamon, fawn.

NOTE

A necklace is the appearance of darker markings encircling the neck. The necklace is not always complete.

Above: The "ambling walk" is reminiscent of her wild relatives; the medium-long legs are powerful and muscular.

Below: The elegant neck blends into a long, powerful body with a slightly rounded rib cage.

Egyptian Mau

Granddaughter of the Marble Legend

She is intended to be the reincarnation of the Egyptian god–cat, Bastet, immortalized in tomb paintings, sculptures, and cat mummies. In spite of a striking resemblance, some claim that she is much more like a wild African cat.

ORIGIN

While it is very unlikely that today's Egyptian Mau is actually a descendant of her ancient namesake (Mau is Egyptian for cat), one of her great-great grandmothers, nevertheless, came from a breed that lived in Cairo in the 1950s. She was brought to Italy, where she was paired with a male cat that also came from Egypt. The offspring were again paired with their parents and those kittens were exported to the United States to breeders who were determined to recreate the ancient Bastet.

Abyssinian, Oriental Shorthair, and the American Shorthair added to the gene pool of these young animals with the Egyptian–Italian history. It was not until 1958, however, that this breed—in type and temperament—satisfied the desire of the Mau fans. The Egyptian Mau only very recently received recognition in Europe from TICA, in 1992.

Above: The eyes of the Egyptian Mau are a light gooseberry-green color.

Left above: Egyptian Mau with bronze spots; the undercoat has an almost golden color, but the neck and underbelly are ivory colored.

Left below: The silver Egyptian Mau displaying the distinctive "mascara" line, extending from the outer corner of the eye.

Left page: Spotted black patterning on the silver ground color is clearly defined for this silver Egyptian Mau. The characteristic M-shaped marking on the forehead is also visible.

Above: The inside of the ear has a shell-pink color and looks almost translucent.

Below: Each hair of the Egyptian Mau has one or two dark bands that are separated by a lighter color.

CHARACTER AND TEMPERAMENT

The spotted Egyptian is a temperamental companion; she is self-assured, critical, intelligent, and loves to be active. She needs lots of space; she is a passionate, eager climber, and talent-

TIPS FOR CARE

If you can manage, try to brush the teeth of your Egyptian Mau twice a week with a special tooth brush to avoid tartar buildup and loss of teeth.

ed jumper. Even as a very young kitten she learns to retrieve a toy in order to entice people to play with her. Human partners are preferred over other animals, which she either tries to dominate or drive out. She seeks human contact (even if not all the time). She belongs to the rare breeds that will without much fuss, for instance, respect the request to stay out of the bedroom or off the bed.

Being alone doesn't bother her, provided her territory offers enough diversion and stimulation. She becomes sullen when confined to a small space. For this reason she should at least have a balcony or a windowsill available to her so she can view the outdoors as well as her indoor world. The Egyptian Mau is somewhat vocal but is generally quiet, with a pleasant, bird-like voice.

TYPE AND STANDARD

TYPE, BODY, LEGS, TAIL

This is an active, gloriously colorful cat of medium size with well-developed muscles. The body is graceful, and one of her characteristic signs is a loose skin fold from the side down to the knees of the hind legs. The hind legs—in relation to the front legs—are longer and give the impression that the cat is standing on tiptoes. The paws are small and delicate and only slightly oval-almost round. The medium-length tail is thick at the base, slightly tapering into a tip.

HEAD, EYES, EARS

The head is slightly rounded without flat planes, and the profile shows a graceful contour with a slight elevation from the bridge of the nose to the forehead. The nose is uniformly wide, the mouth neither short nor pointed. The medium-sized ears should stand alert and be moderately pointed at the tip. The inside of the ears is almost translucent. The hair on the ears is short and close to the skin; the tip of the ears may have small tufts of hair. The large, almond-shaped eyes are set wide apart with a light gooseberry-green color. Kittens' eyes are often amber colored.

COAT

The coat is short but long enough to show two to three tickings with the lighter bands showing; it has a lustrous sheen. Smoke-colored cats have a fine, silk-textured coat; the silver- and bronze-colored are dense, smooth, and resilient.

COLOR

The markings are those of a spotted cat. What follows is a description of only that which is unique and characteristic for this breed. The spots are randomly spread across the body, and varying in size and shape. The spots must be distinct and clearly separated from the base color of the coat. The chest has one or several disrupted necklaces. The stripes on the shoulders change into spots. Along the back the spots are usually elongated and blend into each other at the end of the body to form one line that continues along to the end of the tail. The stripes on the tail are distinct and blend into one color at the tip. The upper part of the front legs has distinct stripes; in the hip area and the upper part of the hind legs the markings show a transition from stripes to spots.

The bronze and silver cats have brick-red nose tips. The black smoke has a black nose tip. The pads are black in a silver and black smoke cat, and in a bronze cat they are dark brown or seal colored.

RECOGNIZED COLOR VARIATIONS

Bronze spotted: almost golden-colored bronze, with ivory-colored neck and underbelly with dark brown or seal-colored spots.

Black-silver spotted: pure silver white; lighter neck and underbelly with black spots.

Black-smoke spotted: smoke colored with cinnamon undercoat; neck and underbelly are lighter, with black spots.

Above: The large, slightly angled eyes are almond shaped.

Below: Neck and underbelly are lighter than the rest of the coat.

Chartreux & Co.

Chartreux

ORIGIN

As is the case with all pure blue cats, this breed could only have been created when its members were isolated from other cat populations, because coat color is only passed on when both parents are purebred.

And such an isolation seems to have been provided during the 12th century in the monastery of La Grande Chartreuse near Grenoble in the French Alps. The Carthusian monks in the cloister used cats to control the rat population and it seems that the cats had no contact with "native" animals—because they were and have always remained blue.

These blue purebred cats still existed in France in the 1930s when breeding enthusiasts discovered them, and from then on bred them as a breed. The British worked hard to cultivate their own Blue and so have been reluctant to

Left page: This oldest breed of all blue cats is a rarity today.

Below: The coat of the Chartreux cat, due to its undercoat, is fur-like and slightly woolly.

recognize this traditional French breed. Two separate lines have thus been bred: the British and the French.

The British Blue is considered an individual breed in Britain. In the United States the Blue is just one of the British Shorthairs.

TYPE AND STANDARD

This cat must be distinctly different from the Russian Shorthair Blue and the British Shorthair Blue. Crossbreeding is not allowed.

TYPE, BODY, LEGS, TAIL

A medium-sized to large cat with strong, solid, muscular body; a wide, well-developed chest; sturdy legs of medium length; and medium-long, but well-rounded tail.

HEAD, EARS, EYES

The head is a large, broad, trapezoidal shape, wide at the base and narrower on top, with a wide, straight nose and medium-sized ears on top of the head. The eyes are large and rounded, the lids slightly pulled upward at the outer corner. The eyes must orange with no hint of green, a lively dark yellow to golden-copper.

RECOGNIZED COLORS

All shades of blue; ideal is light blue-gray.

Above: The head should be a large, broad, trapezoidal shape. The ears, pointed and upright, give the Chartreux an expression of attentiveness.

Right: The Carthusian Chartreux does not have the fat cheeks of the British Shorthair Blue.

CHARACTER AND TEMPERAMENT

The Chartreux is rather reserved; she needs her own space and prefers to live autonomously within her family of people. She loves to be outdoors, and is an enthusiastic and successful hunter. Nevertheless, she distinguishes herself by her faithful attachment to home—she hates moving. She loves to curl up in a lap and be spoiled by those who give her plenty of freedom. During play, she can tell whether she is being teased or is dealing with a serious competitor.

Korat

ORIGIN

This ancient natural breed is indigenous to northern Thailand, named after the province of Korat. Most delicate among the blue cats, she is referred to in Thailand today by her native name "Si-Sawat," which means "the colorful one who brings luck and wealth." The breed has been depicted in Thai painting and poetry, including the *Cat Book Poems* of the Ayutthaya Kingdom (A.D. 1350–1767).

At the end of the nineteenth century, along with Siamese and Burmese a few blue cats also came to England. However, because the blue-eyed Siamese was then considered to be much more spectacular, the others quickly disappeared. It was not until the 1960s that Americans developed a passion for the Korat, starting an association to preserve the original Korat cat. Before the 1980s no more than 1500 animals lived outside Thailand, but by 1983 the breed was recognized by TICA.

CHARACTER AND TEMPERAMENT

This highly perceptive and intelligent cat is considered by some to be the most gentle among the Orientals. While she does not have the fragile body of a Siamese or

Above: The coat of the Korat is silver-blue, tipped with silver, without shading or tabby markings.

Below: The large, prominent eyes are a luminous green, dominating the graceful face of the Korat. A cast of amber to the eyes is acceptable.

Right: Looked at straight-on, the head of the Korat is heart shaped, the ears are large, and the inside of the ear is slightly covered with hair. The nose is dark blue or lavender.

Below: The Korat is a strong, muscular, but graceful cat with a medium-sized build and a somewhat rounded back. The nose shows a slight stop. A stop is an alteration to the nose profile other than straight; also known as a break.

Oriental Shorthair, she nevertheless has much of their temperament.

She bonds extremely closely with people, needs lots of attention, and is possessive. The Korat loves to talk and does a lot of it, but her voice is not as loud as that of her "cousins." She is agile, loves to play, and needs lots of exercise. She can keep a table-tennis ball in motion for hours, and she chases furry toy mice with enthusiasm.

TYPE AND STANDARD

TYPE, BODY, LEGS, TAIL

A medium-sized, alert cat that is muscular, agile, and powerful but not heavy, with well-proportioned legs, where the hind legs are somewhat longer than those in front. The medium-long tail is strong at the root, tapering, and rounded at the tip.

HEAD, EYES, EARS

The face is heart shaped; the nose shows a slight stop and at the tip is turned slightly upward (lion-like). The large, round eyes have a luminous green color. The ears are large, wide at the base, and slightly rounded at the tip. The inside of the ear is covered with hair, the outside generously covered with short hair, flat against the skin.

COAT

The short to medium-long coat, without undercoat, is close to the body, glossy, silky, soft, and fine and has a tendency to break along the spine when the cat is moving.

COLOR

The coat of the Korat cat is always silver-blue, each hair tipped with silver.

Sokoke

ORIGIN

In 1979 on her cocoa plantation in Kenya, Jenny Slater, originally from England, discovered as her gardener was mowing a meadow a black-brown mother cat which—together with her three kittens—had been hiding in a hole. The mother disappeared with the largest and the two siblings were taken into the house. Once they became tame, Mrs. Slater bred them with black house cats and established the Sokoke breed, bringing it to Europe in 1984.

CHARACTER AND TEMPERAMENT

Given her short history as a pet, the Sokoke is surprisingly fond of people, devoted, and always looking for contact. Unlike most other domestic breeds, she shows signs of a hospitable feline social life: Sokoke cats share their prey with each other, hunt as a team, and also share other tasks. Their voice is quiet but they are nevertheless quite vocal to each other and towards people.

Short, glossy coat without an undercoat. Rather than spots, there are distinct tread-like markings—characteristic of the Sokoke.

TYPE AND STANDARD

TYPE, BODY, LEGS, TAIL

A medium-sized slender, muscular cat with a strong bone structure, and a well-developed chest. It has long, slender legs where the hind legs are angled and longer than those in front. The tail is medium long.

HEAD, EYES, EARS

The wedge-shaped head has an almost flat forehead, the medium-long straight nose is wide. The slightly rounded tips of the medium-sized ears have small hair tufts. The large, slightly almond-shaped eyes are wide at the base and a luminous amber-yellow to green.

COAT

The coat is very short, close to the body, glossy but not silky. There is little or no undercoat.

COLORS

The Sokoke has patched tabby with agouti markings in the darker part of the coat.

Recognized color varieties: All shades from black to tabby.

TIPS FOR CARE

The very fine coat is no protection against cold and wet weather. It is essential that a warm place is always available to her.

NOTE

A patched tabby is essentially a torbie—a tortoiseshell tabby.

Bobtail, Manx

Japanese Bobtail

ORIGIN

Since antiquity the Bobtail, considered to bring good fortune, has been the subject of Japanese paintings, carvings, and statues. The first known imports to the United States of Japanese bobtailed cats are in 1908. It was not until the post–World War II era, however, that American servicemen stationed in Japan rediscovered and brought to the United States this living image of antiquity. First shown in the United States in 1968, the breed was recognized in America in 1971. The Japanese Bobtail is rare in Europe and virtually unknown in England.

Whereas Asian cats with stubby and kinked tails may share a common ancestry of more than 1000 years, there is no connection to the Manx; they are separate mutations.

CHARACTER AND TEMPERAMENT

The Japanese Bobtail is a very well-adjusted cat, reserved towards strangers, but never dismissive or mistrusting. She does not bond very quickly, but when she does it is for the duration. She needs a lot of space to play, does well if kept alone, and does not need constant contact with people.

Above: The body of a Japanese Bobtail is long, slender, and elegant, with legs longer in the back than in the front.

Left: Black-white Japanese Bobtail: the black markings should be as dramatic as possible.

Below: Three-colored Japanese Bobtail, the Mi-Ke, with a well-developed pom-pom; the tail hair is longer than the coat of the body.

Left page: The Rumpy Riser Manx has a powerful body.

Left: A rarity—a red-white Japanese Bobtail with blue eyes.

Right: When extended, the tail can be longer than four inches (10 cm), but is usually carried turned under.

She creates games and hunting activities, and when she needs attention she will make it known.

The stumped tail is no disadvantage; she balances as successfully as her long-tailed cousins.

NOTE

Odd-eyed indicates eyes of different colors, typically blue and orange.

TIPS FOR CARE

The turned-under tail stump should be surrounded by feathery, long hair and look like a pom-pom. The coat should be combed daily with a fine-toothed comb.

TYPE AND STANDARD

TYPE, BODY, LEGS, TAIL

A medium-sized cat with a long, elegant body, long, slender legs, the hind legs being distinctly longer than the front, and strongly angled. The short tail should look like a rabbit tail with upright hair like a fan, giving it a pom-pom effect that cover the underlying bone structure. When extended, the bone of the tail measures about 2 to 3 inches (5 to 8 cm) from the body, the fully extended tail bone measuring as much as 5 inches (13 cm).

HEAD, EYES, EARS

The head has the shape of an equilateral triangle, with high cheek bones and a long nose. The ears are large, upright, and wide at the base. The eyes are large, oval, slightly slanted, and may be blue, orange, or odd.

COAT

The fur is of medium length, soft, silky, without a discernible undercoat and with minimal shedding.

COLOR

The preferred color of this breed is that of the Mi-Ke cat: three-colored black, red and white tortoiseshell. In all two- or three-colored cats a primary color may dominate. The contrast of the colors should be strong, sharp, and dramatic.

RECOGNIZED COLOR VARIATIONS

White, black, black tortie, black and white, red and white, black tortie and white (Mi-ke), solid blue and cream, tortie blue-cream.

Tabby: black striped, blue striped, red striped, cream striped, tortie striped, blue tortie striped, silver striped. With white: blue, cream, blue tortie.

Tabby with white.

Manx

ORIGIN

Known on the Isle of Man, between England and Ireland, for centuries, these tailless cats are at once one of the oldest known breeds and the subject of many legends. Since the absence of a tail is a latent gene, the crossing of two tailless cats will produce either no kittens or still-birth. Survival of the breed was possible only after a few animals with more than half carrying the tailless gene came to the Isle of Man—which had been an island without cats. Cat lorists believe the breed is descended from particular cats that swam ashore from a shipwrecked Spanish galleon in 1588.

To this day, each Manx litter produces a tailless (Rumpy) cat as well as those with a hint of a tail (Rumpy-riser) and those with the beginning of a tail (Stumpy), as well as cats with a normal tail (Longy).

CHARACTER AND TEMPERAMENT

The Manx is at the same time an independent as well as a very devoted cat. Her territory is relatively small. She does not show a very developed need for freedom but rather loves her "own four walls." She cuddles with self-abandon and also enjoys "heeling" when going for a walk.

The Rumpy Manx has no trace of tail and has difficulty climbing and jumping. Every Manx loves to play with people. The voice is quiet and pleasant, but is seldom used. Manx cats are very possessive. They really don't like to share their love for people with other cats and have fits of jealousy if their people pay attention to other creatures.

TYPE AND STANDARD

TYPE, BODY, LEGS, TAIL

A sturdily constructed cat with a short back and deep flanks of medium size. The rump is extremely round and wide. The muscular legs are longer in the back than in the front. Rumpy: the tail is missing, the end of the spine has a hole. Rumpy-riser: the spine is extended at the base of the tail and bent slightly upward. Stumpy: the tail is one to two inches (3 to 4 cm) long.

HEAD, EYES, YEARS

The large head is round, the cheeks chubby and pronounced. The nose is of medium length, without a break. The ears are of medium size, ending in a tip, and are placed high on the head. The eyes are large, round, and may be of any color.

COAT

The coat is short and glossy, with an unusual soft and thick double coat.

COLORS

All colors and patterns are allowed.

Top: The Manx developed through incest on the Isle of Man. Rumpy Riser; the tail can be as long as 2 inches (5 cm).

Middle: Rumpy Manx with tail missing.

Bottom: Manx cats can be any color.

European Shorthair

The Barn Kitten with a Gallery of Ancestors

Making a virtue out of a flaw is what the "inventor" was able to do with this breed, because until recently the European Shorthair was nothing more than any domestic cat kept as a household pet, having a family tree that only became "aristocratic" as the cats became rare. Cats have been kept on mainland Europe for thousands of years, but without selective breeding many types, colors, and patterns arose. European Shorthairs, more or less by default, were those cats that had never been introduced to England, where breed standards were subsequently developed.

ORIGIN

To create a breed that would attain a characteristic type reflecting a European street-cat ancestry was the goal of breeders who were able to gain recognition for the breed in its own right only in 1982. Imitating English breeders—who elevated the British Shorthair into the ranks of majestic cats—and the Americans who created the American Shorthair from ordinary house cats—the European breeders wanted to produce a clearly defined type for the European Shorthair: as high-legged and slender as the American, but not quite as round as the British. It

was a cat that Albrecht Dürer had painted, that writers had described in their novels, and that Johann Sebastian Bach had honored in his music.

Above: The coat of the silver shaded has a dark hue.

Left: Silver-striped European Shorthair with a beautiful necklace.

Left page: Cream-colored European Shorthair with deep copper-colored eyes.

TIPS FOR CARE

As a descendant of the original barn cat, the European Shorthair tends towards obesity if she does not get sufficient exercise. Give her only enough food that she will eat in one sitting.

Top right: Snow-white European Shorthair cats are rare.

Below: A house cat with deliberately bred colors: silver tabby European Shorthair.

They soon discovered that this idea was not all that easy to put into practice. In addition, nobody was interested in the breed if it did not have striking colors or markings. Crosses are no longer allowed with the British Shorthair.

CHARACTER AND TEMPERAMENT

Proud, self-assured, independent, the European Shorthair has much in common with her ancestors, but is tending to become less short and compact with a slightly longer

face. She survives beautifully even without human support. She is vibrant, very seldom plagued by pests or illness.

TYPE AND STANDARD

TYPE, BODY, LEGS, TAIL

A robust, agile cat, free of interbreeding. The body is sturdy and muscular with a round, well-developed chest. The legs are strong, powerful, and of medium length and taper evenly down to meet firm, round paws. The medium-length tail, thick at the base, tapers to a rounded tip.

HEAD, EYES, EARS

The large head appears round, has well-developed cheeks and a straight, medium-long nose. The medium-sized ears are slightly rounded at the tip and may have hair tufts that stand upright. The eyes are round, large and expressive, set wide apart and slightly angled; they may be green, yellow, orange, blue, or odd-eyed.

COAT

The coat is short, dense, tight, and shiny.

COLORS

No colors are allowed that are the result of crossbreeding with other breeds.

RECOGNIZED COLOR VARIATIONS

White with blue, green-yellow, or orange eyes. White with odd-eyes.

Solid: black, blue, red, cream.
Tortoiseshell: black, blue.
Smoke: black, blue, red, cream, black tortie, blue tortie.
Tabby: black, blue, red, cream, black tortie, blue tortie.
Silver tabby: black, blue, red, cream, black tortie, blue tortie.
Bicolor: black, blue, red, cream, black tortie, blue tortie.

In addition, she is a very serious cat that—in spite of her permanently childlike expression—would rather hunt than play, but keeps her cousins at a distance. She considers herself the queen of her territory which she will defend fiercely if she feels her domain is not being respected. She loves to be nearby her people without being a pest, but is not lonely by herself.

Above: Blotched tabby is the term for this European Shorthair.

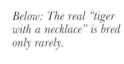

Below: The real "tiger with a necklace" is bred only rarely.

Rex Cats

Gentle Beauties in a Curly Coat

ORIGIN

Chance mutations that happened in different places in plain house and farm cat litters have produced three recognized Rex breeds: the Cornish Rex, the Devon Rex, and the German Rex. Genetically the German and Cornish Rex are related, while the Devon Rex, crossed with another breed with a curly coat, will produce straight-haired kittens—in other words, genetically this breed is not related to the other two.

What Rex cats have in common is their curly coat, where each individual hair is either wavy or curled, including the whiskers—which have corkscrew-like waves. It is possible that such mutations are common; however, they can only be passed on if they are recognized by breeders and specifically paired. The name Rex comes from a similar mutation in rabbits.

The names also indicate where each Rex mutation occurred: the Devon Rex appeared in Devonshire, the Cornish Rex in Cornwall, and the German Rex, of course, in Germany.

CHARACTER AND TEMPERAMENT

All Rex cats have a few things in common: an enchantingly innocent charm with which they approach people, the grace and beauty of their movement, and their insatiable desire for cuddling. Whenever a Rex cat plays on a shelf, nothing will be broken because she is so agile.

They will search for a resting place as close as possible to a human being and/or the fireplace, the radiator, or a sunny windowsill. They are ideal partners in a quiet household where there is always somebody present, and where reading, television watching, and conversations take place. Noises, turbulence, chaos are what these gentle cats try to avoid.

CORNISH REX

A medium-sized cat with a solid, muscular, sleek body, long, straight legs, and small, oval paws. The tail is long, thin, tapering to a point, and well covered with curly fur. The relatively small, wedge-shaped head is narrower towards the chin. The nose is straight, the hair of the whiskers and brows long and curly. The ears are large, covered with fine hair, and set high on the head. The medium-sized, almond-shaped eyes are brilliant and the color is pure and clear. The coat is short and dense, somewhat furry, curled or wavy—particularly on the back and tail—without any guard hairs.

Above: The Cornish Rex (here in cream) has a short, dense, fur-like coat with waves and curls.

Below: The soft and furry coat of the Devon Rex (brown tabby) is very short and fine.

Left page: Tortie smoke Devon Rex, a delicate graceful cat.

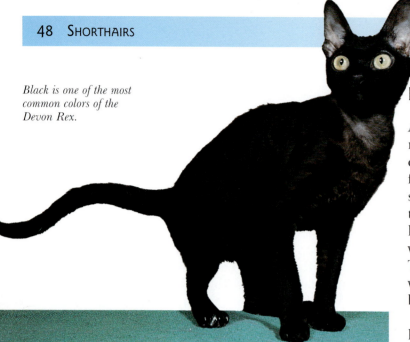

Black is one of the most common colors of the Devon Rex.

DEVON REX

A medium-sized cat with a solid, muscular, sleek body, and a white chest on long slender legs. The front legs angle inward so that a slight O-shape is suggested from the paws to the chest. The tail is long and thin, tapering to the tip, well covered with fine, short fur. The head is shaped like a medium wedge, with protruding cheek bones and a rounded forehead.

The nose is very short; the whiskers and brows are stiff, medium long, and curly. The ears are wide set at the base and taper into a rounded tip. They are well covered with fine hair, with or without a skin fold in the back at the base of the ear. The large, oval eyes are well separated, sloping towards the ears' outer edges, and are brilliant, pure, and clear in color. The coat is very short, fine, soft and wavy, and appears to have no guard hairs, although, down, awn, and guard hairs are all present.

GERMAN REX

A medium-sized cat with a muscular body, strong chest, straight back, and medium-long legs. The tail tapers to a rounded tip, and is

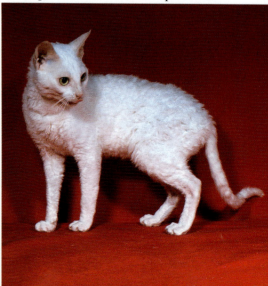

well covered with hair. The head is rounded, with well-developed cheeks and a slight break in the nose. The whiskers are curly and shorter than usual for a cat of this size. Medium-sized ears have rounded tips; the outsides are well covered with hair, the insides only slightly. Medium-sized eyes are alert and brilliant. The short, velvety coat is soft, very silky, and curly or wavy without guard hairs.

RECOGNIZED COLOR VARIATIONS FOR ALL REX BREEDS

Solid/smoke/with white/smoke with white: black, blue, chocolate, lavender, cinnamon, fawn.

Red/cream: solid, striped, piebald, spotted, banded.

Black tortie/blue tortie, chocolate tortie, lilac tortie, cinnamon tortie, fawn tortie: striped, piebald, spotted, banded.

Smoke: red, cream, black tortie, blue tortie, chocolate tortie, lavender tortie, cinnamon tortie, fawn tortie.

Golden shaded/patched/striped/piebald/spotted/banded: red, cream, black tortie, blue tortie, chocolate tortie, lavender tortie, cinnamon tortie, fawn, tortie.

Red with white/cream with white/black tortie with white/blue tortie with white/chocolate tortie with white/lavender tortie with white/cinnamon tortie with white/fawn tortie with white: striped, piebald, spotted, banded.

Smoke with white: red, cream, black tortie, blue tortie, chocolate tortie, lavender tortie, cinnamon tortie, fawn tortie.

Golden shaded/patched/striped/piebald/spotted/banded with white: red, cream, black tortie, blue tortie, chocolate tortie, lavender tortie, cinnamon tortie, fawn tortie.

Black/blue/chocolate/lavender/cinnamon/-fawn: striped, piebald, spotted, banded.

Silver shaded/patched/striped/piebald/spotted/banded: black, blue, chocolate, lavender, red, cream, cinnamon, fawn, black tortie, blue tortie, chocolate tortie, lavender tortie, cinnamon tortie, fawn tortie.

Golden/shaded/patched/striped/piebald/spotted/banded: black, blue, chocolate, lavender, cinnamon, fawn.

Striped/spotted/piebald/banded with white: black, blue, chocolate, lavender, cinnamon, fawn.

Silver shaded/patched/striped/piebald/spotted/banded with white: black, blue, chocolate, lavender, red, cream, cinnamon, fawn, black tortie, blue tortie, chocolate tortie, lavender tortie, cinnamon tortie, fawn tortie.

Golden shaded/patched/striped/piebald/spotted/banded with white: black, blue, chocolate, lavender, cinnamon, fawn.

White pointed (Siamese markings): black, blue, chocolate, lavender, red, cream, cinnamon, fawn, black tortie, blue tortie, chocolate tortie, lavender tortie, cinnamon tortie, fawn tortie.

Pointed tabby/pointed silver/pointed silver tabby: black, blue, chocolate, lavender, red, cream, cinnamon, fawn, black tortie, blue tortie, chocolate tortie, lavender tortie, cinnamon tortie, fawn tortie.

Pointed golden/pointed golden tabby: black, blue, chocolate, lavender, red, cream, cinnamon, fawn, black tortie, blue tortie, chocolate tortie, lavender tortie, cinnamon tortie, fawn tortie.

Pointed with white, pointed tabby with white: black, blue, chocolate, lavender, red, cream, cinnamon, fawn, black tortie, blue tortie, chocolate tortie, lavender tortie, cinnamon tortie, fawn tortie.

Pointed silver with white, pointed silver tabby with white, pointed golden with white, pointed golden tabby with white: black, blue, chocolate, lavender, red, cream, cinnamon, fawn, black tortie, blue tortie, chocolate tortie, lavender tortie, cinnamon tortie, fawn tortie.

TIPS FOR CARE

The curly coat itself needs no care; however, a Rex cat is particularly in need of warmth. It should be provided with a place that is closed, well padded, soft, and cuddly where it can withdraw when things get too hectic or too cold.

NOTE

Guard hairs form the top-coat; down hair is the soft, short secondary hairs; and awn hairs are a coarser form of secondary hair, with thickened tips.

Previous page, below left: Si-Rex is the name of this Devon Rex with Siamese markings.

Previous page, below right: The coat of the German Rex is denser than that of its English relatives.

Burmese

A Golden-Eyed Hobgoblin with a Velvety Coat

She talks and laughs, she sighs and curses, she resists any attempt to be trained—but in spite of it all, she captivates every person of her choosing. The Burmese cat, a close relative to the Siamese, will lift her mysterious veil only in small increments.

ORIGIN

A ship's surgeon, Dr. Joseph Thompson, brought a cat named "Wong Mau" to America along with a blue-eyed Siamese from Rangoon, the capital of Burma (Myanmar). He referred to her as "my little brown kitten." This small, brown cat had a very special silky, short coat, but with darker markings on head, legs, and tail. Dr. Thompson crossed her with excellent-quality Siamese and the litter included "purebred" Siamese kittens as well as the "Browns."

Within four years the CFA recognized the Burmese as an independent breed. The English had much earlier, in the late nineteenth century, brought both blue-eyed Siamese as well as yellow-eyed Browns to London. But the Browns were of no interest to breeders and disappeared into private hands without leaving any descendants. The fate of "Wong Mau" was quite different, as she stands as the ancestor of all Burmese cats alive today. There is evidence to suggest that "Wong Mau" was actually an intermediate hybrid between Siamese and Burmese, which is now recognized in the United States and Canada as Tonkinese.

CHARACTER AND TEMPERAMENT

The Burmese has a large vocabulary, with which she questions, answers, encourages, comforts, reprimands, says thank you, expresses joy and frustration—the Burmese chatters constantly but very quietly. Her meows are a constant companion to people from the moment they get up in the morning until they retire at night, where the soft chatter subsides into a steady purr. A Burmese is either in a particularly good mood or just as easily very moody, but only for a short while. She enjoys her life in an almost child-like and enthusiastic fashion, where everything new and exciting is greeted with joy and humor.

Above: Light, delicately dove-blue with a slight pink shimmer: these are the colors of the coat of the Lilac Burmese.

Center left: Silky-haired, with a beautiful coat: the Burmese cat—here in blue—is very much like her oriental cousin; however, she is not as slender as the Siamese.

Left page: The eyes should be a brilliant amber.

People as well as animals are welcome in the household. Even when she is fully grown it seems that she can never get enough of playing. What she likes are both places where there is lots going on and places where she can retreat, such as under the bed covers, to take a warm, cozy nap.

TIPS FOR CARE

Due to their temperament, Burmese cats need a very solid scratching post and cat "tree"—if possible with several different levels and hiding places where little balls or other toys are suspended on elastic.

TYPE AND STANDARD

TYPE, BODY, LEGS, TAIL

An elegant exotic cat, medium-sized with a solid, compact muscular body, rounded chest, and straight back. The legs are slender, the tail is medium long, thick at the base and tapering slightly to a rounded tip.

HEAD, EYES, EARS

The head tapers to a blunt wedge, is slightly rounded on top, and has wide-set cheek bones. The ears are broad at the base with rounded tips. Set wide apart, eyes are large, brilliant, amber to golden-yellow.

COAT

The satin coat is fine, glossy, short, close to the body, and has almost no undercoat.

COLOR

Burmese occur in a number of colors, regardless of which registry accepts what.

RECOGNIZED COLOR VARIATIONS

Sable is the color in the United States, with blue, champagne, and platinum registered separately as Malayan. In Britain, the above colors are all Burmese. Further colors recognized in Britain are: cream, red, brown tortie, blue-cream tortie, chocolate tortie, and lilac-cream tortie (described as lavender-cream tortie in the United States).

Above right: Blue-gray with a cinnamon-colored glow: the blue Burmese.

Center right: Light apricot-colored cream Burmese with a powder-colored tint.

Right: Warm seal (black-brown) is the color of the Sable Burmese. This is the traditional color of the breed, known in Britain as the "Brown."

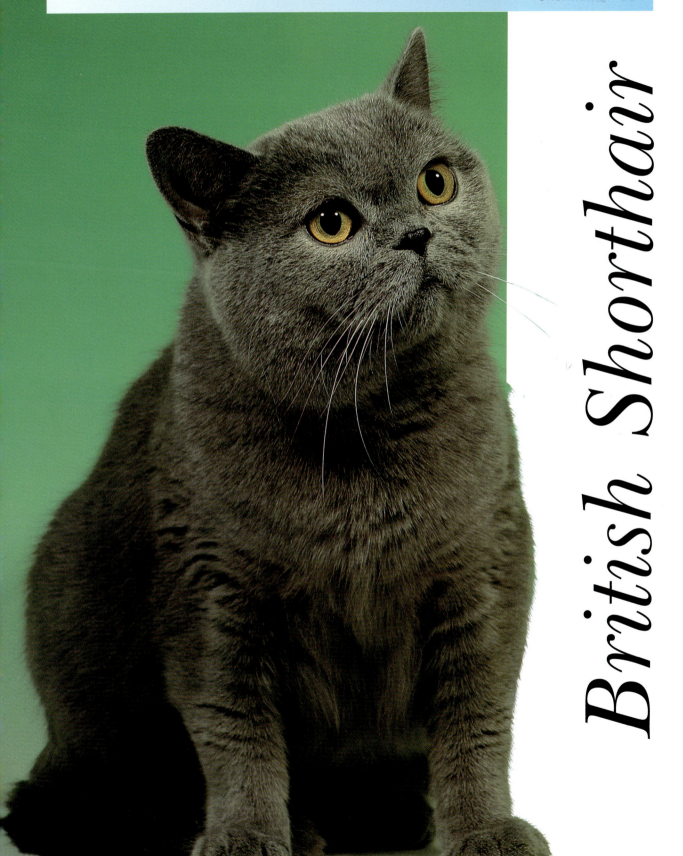

British Shorthair

Preceding page: Stocky, round, and cuddly. It was the Persian that gave the British Shorthair her solid, cobby shape.

A Furry Princess without Affectations

Above: British Shorthairs can also be snow-white.

Below: Red tabby British Shorthair—the eyes are a brilliant dark orange.

Cuddly, comfy, with a fleecy fur, but without the urgent need for the outdoors like her ancestors, the British Shorthair has been able to purr her way to the top of the breeds. Particularly the blue variety is among the most favorite of all short-haired cats.

ORIGIN

Considered the oldest natural English breed, the British Shorthair may have descended from the rugged street cats brought on the shoulders of Roman soldiers. Today, she owes her existence to the pride of early English breeders, to whom it was important that all pets conformed to a standard appearance while showing as many color variations as possible. With much pride, some breeders, such as cat fancier Harrison Weir, showed their ordinary domestic cats during the earliest cat exhibitions in the late nineteenth century. As early as 1911 a British Blue was awarded the much-sought-after trophy for Best in Show, which —on the European continent— was exclusively reserved for Persians or Siamese. Through cross-breeding with Persians, the British Shorthair developed more fullness of the body and head, and became the cobby (chubby, compact) cat that is still such a favorite today.

CHARACTER AND TEMPERAMENT

"All around problem-free cat" could be the name of this British example—she is friendly, cuddly, robust, companionable, gets along with other cats and other pets in the house, loves children, doesn't whine, and is ready to play at any time. She is just as satisfied to curl up on your lap or join her people watching TV. Of course, like all cats, she has her own mind and knows how to assert herself.

While her need for outside activity has long been replaced by contentment in being in the house, this cat—which can hardly be called delicate—needs plenty of space. Especially when involved in a "phantom hunt" she chases her imaginary prey with gusto and surprising agility.

TYPE AND STANDARD

TYPE, BODY, LEGS, TAIL

Large with a wide chest, short legs, and a short, thick tail with a slightly rounded tip.

HEAD, EYES, EARS

The head is wide, round and massive with a straight nose that has a slight indentation. The ears are small and a bit rounded. The large, round eyes are set well apart; their color may be gold, copper, green, blue-green, hazel, or odd-eyed—blue with orange, copper, or golden.

COAT

The short, dense coat is fine textured and fluffy with a well-developed undercoat.

COAT COLOR

Except for the tabby varieties, each hair should have a uniform color to the tip.

RECOGNIZED COLOR VARIATIONS

White with blue, orange, or odd-colored eyes.

Solid with copper or orange colored eyes: black, blue, chocolate, lilac, red, cream.

Tortoiseshell with copper or orange eyes: white, black, blue, chocolate, lilac.

Smoke with copper or orange eyes: black, blue, chocolate, lilac, red, cream, black tortie, blue tortie, chocolate tortie, lilac tortie.

Silver shaded/shell with green or blue eyes respectively, copper or orange colored eyes respectively: black, blue, chocolate, lilac, red, cream, black tortie, blue tortie, chocolate tortie, lilac tortie. Golden shaded/shell with green or blue eyes respectively black outline around the eyes and black tipping on the hairs.

Non-silver tabby with copper or orange eyes: black tabby, blue tabby, chocolate tabby, lilac tabby, red tabby, cream tabby, black tortie tabby, blue tortie tabby, chocolate tortie tabby, lilac tortie tabby.

Silver tabby with green eyes: black, blue, chocolate, lilac, red, cream, black tortie, blue tortie, chocolate tortie, lilac tortie. Golden tabby with green or blue-green eyes outlined in black and black tabby markings.

Van/Harlequin/Bicolor: black, blue, chocolate, lilac, red, cream, black tortie, blue tortie, chocolate tortie, lilac tortie.

Newly recognized in 1991, in Britain only, are the Color Pointed British Shorthairs—entirely different than the similarly named Colorpoint Shorthairs of the United States.

TIPS FOR CARE

Adult animals prefer a large covered litter box that is placed in a quiet corner of the house.

Left: The well-bodied single coat is short and dense.

Below: Perhaps the most popular of all short-haired breeds, the original coat color: the British Blue.

Abyssinian

Grace with the Look of a Puma

She is believed by some to be one of the oldest breeds of domestic cat, but her past is shrouded in darkness. She was nicknamed over 120 years ago as "Child of the Gods," not just because of her luminescent light-reflecting coat, but also because of her radiant, enchanting, and warm-hearted temperament.

ORIGIN

British officers returning from the Abyssinian War in 1868 brought many feline souvenirs of a gold-brown cat with amber-colored eyes to London from what is today Ethiopia. And ever since, speculation abounds about the origin of this cat, first called the British Ticked, with the beautiful coat that resembles the African wild cat (*Felis libyca*) and the cats of ancient Egypt. Researchers went to Ethiopia and were unable to find street cats with the characteristic agouti markings, but eventually they found them in India. And it still remains a mystery if the cats, called bunny cats, with their "rabbit" coats were brought to Ethiopia from India on merchant, or war, ships.

Fanciers prefer the idea of an ancient origin. While the breed is, indeed, "ancient" and "pure" compared to many others, it owes

its present form to the selective breeding practices of early British fanciers rather than a direct, uninterrupted line. In 1871, at the Crystal Palace in London, the first Abyssinian was shown, and as early as 1882 the breed was recognized. A year later the standard for the "bunny cat" was established. And it has remained unchanged; only a few additional colors have been added—today's Abyssinians are almost identical to those first introduced.

CHARACTER AND TEMPERAMENT

When an Abyssinian shows interest in a person—it's all over, because nobody can resist her charm and determination. Whenever she wants to capture a person's heart, the Aby can be unbelievably intense and energetic. She pulls out all stops: she woos, purrs, follows every step, snuggles, nudges with her nose a person's neck or legs.

Above left: A warm blue-gray with dark, steel-blue ticking and a blue-gray outline around the eyes.

Above right: Two to three stripes on each hair and dark tips result in an agouti coat (here a Sorrel).

Above: The underbelly, chest, and inside of legs are the same color.

Left page: The red Aby is Sorrel: copper red with chocolate-colored ticking.

The eyes are large, almond shaped, and amber, green, or hazel.

Once successful, she shows her happiness clearly but very quietly. She asks for attention with a gentle pleasant voice.

TIPS FOR CARE

The coat of the Abyssinian can be even more brilliant and intense if it receives sufficient sunlight. Make sure, therefore, that your Aby has a place on a windowsill—better yet, outside on a balcony or terrace.

TYPE AND STANDARD

TYPE, BODY, LEGS, TAIL

An agile cat of medium size that is wiry but still elegant, and with long legs and a long tail tapering to the tip.

HEAD, EARS, EYES

The head is wedge shaped with soft, graceful contours, medium-long nose, and a powerful, well-developed chin. The ears are relatively large, wide at the base, and slightly rounded at the tip with a thumb print on the back and preferably a tuft of hair on the tip. The large almond-shaped eyes are set wide apart and are of luminous amber, green, or hazel with outlines in the color of the ticking.

COAT

The coat is short, fine, dense, and close to the body.

COLOR

The coat has two or three bands on each hair with the tip of each hair shaded dark.

RECOGNIZED COLOR VARIATIONS

Wild colors: the undercoat is dark apricot-orange, the topcoat a warm reddish brown with black ticking, black at the tip of the ears, tip of the tail, and around the eyes; the nose is brick-red, sometimes framed; the pads are black.

Blue: the undercoat is light beige, the coat a warm blue-gray with dark steel-gray ticking; there is a blue-gray outline around the eyes, and a pink nose with or without an outline around it—and pink/blue-gray pads.

Sorrel: base color is dark-apricot, the coat a brilliant warm copper-red with chocolate-brown ticking, red-brown outline around the eyes, pink nose with or without red-brown outline, cinnamon to chocolate color pads.

Beige-fawn: the base color is light cream; the coat is a dull, faintly beige color with dark, warm, cream ticking; there is a darker fawn outline around the eyes and a pink nose with or without an outline—and pink pads.

Silver: black silver, blue silver, sorrel silver, beige-fawn silver (basic color always pure silver-white, coat silver-white with ticking in the respective colors).

Somali

Noble Grace
with a Silken Stole

For a few engaged breeders it was at first chance—but later an obsession: breeding a long-haired variety of the Abyssinian with a similarly distinctive coat. No one could have imagined the result: the Somali became a big hit and an agouti boom began.

ORIGIN

Some believe, but others vehemently deny, that a Persian or Angora long-haired cat must have been crossed with the Abyssinian to create the Somali. However, it had long been known that among a purebred Abyssinian's litter there appeared kittens with longer hair around the shoulders, loins, and tail. At first these kittens were quietly ignored and not spoken of until—in the 1960s—an American fancier developed the breed and presented her cats to the public. She searched for other Abyssinian owners who had also found these long-haired cats occurring among their litters. After only seven years from her first public requests, she founded the Somalian Cat Club and gave the breed its name (after Somalia, bordering Ethiopia—formerly Abyssinia—in Africa). In

Top left: A delicate, very dense coat with a soft texture is characteristic of the Somali. The ruff and "pants" should be full.

Above: The ears have large tufts at the tip.

Right: The hair on the long, tapering tail of the Somali should be particularly long and delicate.

Previous page: The coat around the shoulders is not as long as on the rest of the body.

1978 the Somali was officially recognized by the CFA, and today is one of the public's favorite breeds at every exhibition.

CHARACTER AND TEMPERAMENT

The character of the Somali is much like her Abyssinian sister—only somewhat more moderate and maybe a little more stubborn. A Somali will show patience; she can wait and simply sit out a confrontation with her owner. Most of the time she gets her way, but, she is not quite as arrogant or unreserved towards strangers as the Aby.

She develops a deep, close relationship—laden with jealousy—to the person she has chosen. She will not easily share favors her owner bestows on her, and will quickly put herself into the foreground and—without much fuss—push any rival decidedly out of the way.

She loves playing just like the Abyssinian, however, she is not very eager to be outdoors. She is most happy with a secure place in the warm sun on a balcony or in front of a large window.

TYPE AND STANDARD

TYPE, BODY, LEGS, TAIL

An agile, muscular cat of medium size, with a graceful neck, wiry, long legs, and small oval paws. The long, tapering tail is well covered with hair.

HEAD, EARS, EYES

The head is wedge-shaped with a medium-long nose. The large ears are set wide apart with a thumb print on the back and tufts on the rounded tips. The large, almond-shaped eyes are set wide apart.

COAT

The coat is soft, very fine and dense. It is generally of medium length, except on the shoulders, where it may be short. Long hair on the hind quarters gives the appearance that she is "wearing pants," and the neck is similarly covered with a dense ruff.

COLORS

The ticking in Somalis develops over a period of two years, but then every individual hair should show two or three colored bands and be dark at the tip.

RECOGNIZED COLOR VARIATIONS

Body and base color as well as the outline around the eyes, the tip of the nose, and the pads have the same coloring as those on the Abyssinian color variations.

Non-silver: ruddy, red, blue, sorrel, lavender, blue-cream.

Silver: ruddy silver, blue-silver, sorrel-silver, cream-silver, chocolate-silver.

TIPS FOR CARE

Somalis love and need to be combed. Use a wide-toothed comb once daily for the ruff, pants, and the tail.

Left: Because of their medium-long, dense coat Somalis do not appear to be as slender as their short-haired sisters, the Abyssinians.

Below: The neck and belly coloration reflects that of the underlying base hair; here a rich shade of cream in this Blue-Cream Somali.

Turkish Van

White-Red Water Nymph with Strong Character

She was first hailed as the "swimming beauty," discovered in the remote Van Lake district of Turkey.

There she lived in small groups. These cats with their medium-long hair and extraordinary markings were only brought to England by tourists in 1955, and then later also to the European continent. To this day they are quite rare, yet famous for their love of water.

ORIGIN

Most likely the Turkish Van is a descendant of the Turkish Angora, having developed as a natural breed when individual Angoras established themselves around Van Lake. Since this body of water is surrounded by mountains, the cat population that developed was isolated from the rest of the world—the best conditions for a mutation to take place.

The Van has very characteristic coat markings that are quite different from, but in the same manner as, the Siamese. The coat is chalk-white with auburn (chestnut-red) or cream markings—colors that could only develop through incest or a very focused breeding program. Even in breeding circles she is still a rarity.

CHARACTER AND TEMPERAMENT

One can sense the centuries-long independence from people in this powerful cat: she is teeming with self-confidence. She loves to be on her own and decides for herself when and with whom she wants to have contact. Nobody can force himself on her, not even with little tidbits, because the Turkish Van is incorruptible.

She needs a lot of free space, preferably outdoors in the garden, because she is still an uncanny and

Above: Chalk-white with no hint of yellow is the requirement for the under-coat of the Turkish Van.

Left: An auburn spot starts at the rump and covers the whole tail, ending in pale stripes of red-cream.

Left page: Even the delicately round paws have dense hair tufts.

able hunter, never deterred by either wind or weather. Watch her carefully: the Turkish Van can catch fish even in the deepest ponds and loves to hunt birds.

The gentle and graceful side of this white-red cat is expressed only to those she feels belong to her. She will follow them through the house, stay close when they rest, squint happily and pay her respects with lots of purring.

TIPS FOR CARE

If her daily life is relatively sedate, this powerful cat tends to become overweight. Make sure therefore that she has enough opportunity for regular exercise and play, time that will use up her excess energies especially if she has no access to the outdoors.

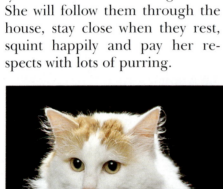

TYPE AND STANDARD

TYPE, BODY, LEGS, TAIL

A cat of medium size with a long, powerful, muscular body, medium-long legs with the hind longer than the fore, and delicate, round paws with tufts between the pads.

HEAD, EYES, EARS

The head is short, slightly wedge shaped with a medium-long straight nose and large ears that are wide at the base and slightly rounded on the tip. The large, oval eyes are set slightly at an angle and may be blue, light amber, or odd-eyed; the eyelids should be outlined in pink.

COAT

The medium-long coat has a fine, silky, texture without a furry undercoat.

COLORS

The ground color is chalk-white without a trace of yellow. The face may have auburn-(chestnut-red) or cream-colored spots with a white blaze; the ears must be white on the outside and faintly pink inside. An auburn or cream-colored spot starts at the rump and covers the entire tail with faint stripes.

RECOGNIZED COLOR VARIATIONS

Auburn with blue, amber, or odd-colored eyes.

Cream with blue, amber, or odd-colored eyes.

Upper right: A rarity: a Turkish Van with blue eyes—which are associated with deafness.

Center: The Turkish Van has no undercoat; the hair is delicate and silky in texture.

Right: The Turkish Van also has auburn or cream spots on her face, but she must always have a white blaze.

Turkish Angora

Comeback of a Servant

Above: The large eyes are almond shaped and slightly angled; they may have all color shades, including amber, blue, green, and hazel.

Right: The original white Turkish Angora is the national cat of Turkey.

Below: White Turkish Angora cats have either blue, amber, or odd-colored eyes—one amber and one blue (right).

Previous page: The body of the Turkish Angora is graceful and sleek.

This oldest of long-haired breeds once rested at the feet of kings and courtiers. She enchanted artists and gave hope to the desperate, and then—during the boom in popularity of Persians—nearly became extinct. The Turkish government set up a breeding program at Ankara Zoo to revive the breed. And it is the descendants of those Ankara Zoo cats that are seen at shows and fascinate people today.

ORIGIN

As early as the end of the 16th century, the Italian adventurer Petro della Valle reported the existence of a long-haired cat that lived in Ankara. During the middle of the 17th century a few of these legendary white cats reached Europe and were named *Catus angorensis* by zoologists—after the region where they lived. They were considered precious and were much sought after, particularly when they had a true snow-white, silky coat. King Louis XV of France made them acceptable at court, and during the 18th century they enjoyed their triumphant presence in almost every European palace.

However, the presence and breeding of Persians—heavier and with a much more luxuriant coat—made the cat from Ankara much less fashionable and breeding was discontinued. Even in Ankara this cat almost disappeared during the chaos of the two World Wars. It was not until the late 1940s that the Turkish government put this cat under protection as a natural treasure. At the beginning of the 1960s the originally

very strict ban on export was partially lifted, and the first Angora cats were allowed to leave the zoo, given into the hands of private breeders in the United States.

In 1973, the Turkish Angora was recognized by the CFA, and by TICA in 1989. Today, the Turkish Angora no longer is restricted to being only snow-white—almost all colors have become allowed.

CHARACTER AND TEMPERAMENT

The Turkish Angora hates to be alone. She loves to bond with people and chatters with them in a pleasant voice. She belongs to the sensitive breeds that abhor noise and commotion; she remains discreetly in the background when strangers are present.

She is playful but does not like rough play; she much prefers retrieving, with great elegance, small balls of crumpled paper. She will cuddle gently in the lap of her favorite person and loves to bat a table tennis ball carefully to send it silently across the floor.

She also makes friends with other pets in the home, and seeks their company without becoming obsessive. Keeping on schedule is important to her, and she trusts her environment—in other words, she is not a cat for hectic people. She hates chaos and commotion, even in her own home. She hides when guests in the house are loud, and she is not the type that will immediately jump into any stranger's lap. Whoever wants to draw her out of her reserved attitude must be peaceful, quiet, and very patient.

TYPE AND STANDARD

TYPE, BODY, LEGS, TAIL

A graceful, supple cat with delicate bone structure, a slender body, somewhat higher in the hindquarters than the front. Toms are larger than the females. The legs are long, the paws are small and delicate, with tufts between the pads. The tail is long and tapers to a tip, wide at the base and narrower at the end and well covered with fur. The tail is carried lower than—not quite parallel to—the back, but it does not drag.

HEAD, EYES, EARS

The head is small and wedge shaped, wide at the upper part and tapering slightly towards the chin, with a medium-long concave nose without a break. The chin is gently rounded. The ears are long, pointed, well covered with hair, and have tufts. The large, almond-shaped eyes are slightly angled and may be of any color, including odd-eyed.

COAT

The coat is medium long around the body and long on the ruff; the hair is very delicate with a silky sheen. The coat on the underbelly is slightly wavy. The ruff is not quite developed during the first year of the cat's life. The winter coat is longer than the summer coat.

COLORS AND COLOR VARIATIONS

All colors are allowed except chocolate, lilac, cinnamon, and fawn. All varieties with white are allowed, with the exception of pointed and tabby striped.

TIPS FOR CARE

The Turkish Angora is very fussy and needs the best possible hygiene. The litter should always be fresh; two litter boxes are best.

Upper right above: The ruff around the neck should be somewhat longer and denser.

Above: The coat is medium long, silky, flowing, and slightly wavy on the underside. The hair is fine, with a silky sheen.

Left: Turkish Angora cats may also be tortoiseshell.

Sacred Birman

A Wise White Cat with a Golden Glow

About as many legends exist about the origin of the Sacred Birman as there are about her unique appearance. But all real attempts to clarify the stories go nowhere. The puzzle about her roots may well remain a mystery forever.

ORIGIN

It is known that in the nineteenth century the French Vice Consul in Luang Prabang and his friend Major Russell Gordon came back to Europe with a blue-eyed ivory-colored cat with a golden sheen in her coat and snow-white paws. They reported that this cat was the mascot of the Kittah Lama of Burma.

With this report also came the legend of "Sinh," the male temple cat that was sitting next to the head priest who was meditating. "Sinh" was white with golden eyes and his paws, ears, and tail were dark. The cat touched the priest as he died during an uprising. It was said that the head priest's soul united with that of "Sinh," and, at that moment, "Sinh's" yellow eyes turned sapphire blue, his body took on a golden sheen, and the paws—which the cat had placed on the head of the priest—became snow-white up to where they were covered by the priest's sacred clothing.

The rebels supposedly became very frightened of this cat-goddess and retreated. "Sinh" had prevented the temple's desecration and plundering. When the priests held a meeting to choose a new head priest, every temple cat came and each had already been transformed the same as "Sinh." To this day this legend is all that is known about the origin of the Sacred Birman. The fate of the cat brought back from Burma by Vice Consul and Major Gordon is unknown.

New Birman cats did not arrive in Europe until 1920, among them a pregnant cat by the name of "Sita." Her descendants ended up in the hands of breeders in France, but it is impossible to trace even how that came to pass. Two animals were shown at the exhibition in Paris for the first time in 1925, and the same year France

Above: Blue tabby kitten; it takes up to two years for the coat to develop into its full splendor.

Left page: The snow-white paws are the classic marking of the Sacred Birman.

Below: Kittens do not yet show their full markings.

Above: A blue tabby Sacred Birman with kittens.

Below: In contrast to the Sacred Birman, the Himalayan—known in Britain as the Colorpoint Persian—has black paws.

recognized them as a distinct breed. Descendants of these two, as well as presumed—but unknown—crossbreeding, established the type. A standard was set in 1955 that recognized this breed worldwide. Only recently has the Sacred Birman been introduced into the United States.

CHARACTER AND TEMPERAMENT

The Sacred Birman—the grande dame among all cat breeds—is a bundle of charm paired with in-comparable elegance and a good dose of self-confidence. With great dignity, she majestically rules the roost, and makes people her servants. Nobody will complain when she decides to initiate a game; nobody can resist when she wants to be cuddled—even if the alarm clock has just announced it is time to get up and go to work. With a gentle voice she will complain when the food is not to her liking, and a quiet singsong will remind the owner that it is time to

clean out her litter box. Her sapphire-blue eyes will give you a reproachful look if you disturb her while she is busy grooming; and her tail will twitch in annoyance to remind you that she wants to be left alone. Some owners of the Sacred Birman insist that their cats have a sense of feline family—that they recognize one another and congregate with members of their breed.

The markings in young Sacred Birmans are still diffused; the coat will need about two years in order to develop into its full splendor.

TYPE AND STANDARD

TYPE, BODY, LEGS, TAIL

A medium-sized cat with a long body, short, powerful legs, and rounded paws with a medium-long tail with a feathery tip.

HEAD, EARS, EYES

The forehead is slightly rounded, the cheeks are full, the nose is medium long without a stop, but with a slight indentation. The ears are relatively small, but medium long, and have rounded tips; the eyes are just slightly oval and of a brilliant deep blue.

COAT

The coat is long to medium long, short around the face, where it increases towards the cheeks, blending into a full collar. The coat is long on the back and the flanks. It has a silky texture and very little undercoat.

COLORS

The Birman has the same characteristic coat coloring as the Colorpoint Shorthairs; however, all four legs are white (mittens). Their points stretch over the face, ears, legs, tail, and genitals. They must be uniform in color and contrast clearly. The body color is light, eggshell; the back is golden-beige.

The paws in front as well as back are called mittens and must be pure white. The white color should stop at the joint or the point where the toes end and the metacarpals begin. On the hind paws the laces end in a tip—ideally, in an upside-down "V"—and reaches halfway or more up to the heel.

RECOGNIZED COLOR VARIATIONS

Seal point, blue point, chocolate point, and lilac point, as well as red point, cream point, seal tortie point, blue tortie point, chocolate tortie point, lilac tortie point.

Tabby point: seal, blue, chocolate, and lilac, as well as red, cream, seal tortie, blue tortie, chocolate tortie, and lilac tortie.

NOTE

Laces is the term for the white fur extending from the paws up the hind legs of the Sacred Birman.

Ragdoll

Little Doll and Mascot

She is the invention out of the imagination of a breeder who wanted a cat that was more gentle and snuggly than those she had up till then. And that's why the breeder gave this mixed breed the name Ragdoll, a term that created much prejudice—something that has not been overcome to this day.

like a wet rag, and lacked any sense of themselves, having no mind of their own. Only about 15 years ago, after the first Ragdolls came to Europe, were all these rumors proved wrong; these cats behaved just like any normal domestic cat—with some traits that could be found in a variety of breeds. Meanwhile, a standard was established, and this breed was recognized in the United States in 1965 and by international associations in 1983.

ORIGIN

Ann Baker, from Riverside, California, had enough scratches on her arms and legs, or so the story goes. She was longing for cats that would never tire of cuddling, that would be gentle but still robust. She began to experiment, breeding many different cats as long as they had one of the desired characteristics. She chose the name Ragdoll because the cats became extraordinarily relaxed, like limp ragdolls, when lifted or stroked by their owners. The reaction to the Ragdoll cat was a great deal of astonishment and amused laughter—but also a great many insults. Malicious rumors had it that these animals had absolutely no temperament, were impervious to pain, could be dragged around

Left page: Large, compact paws and dense tufts between the toes are the mark of the Ragdoll.

Left: The coat around the neck is long, framing the face.

Below: The Ragdoll is one of the largest cat breeds; a male cat weighing 22 pounds (10 kg) is not uncommon.

CHARACTER AND TEMPERAMENT

This is a cat of infinite docility and gentleness. Although she is powerful and strong, she almost never uses her claws, and will only become aggressive when she feels threatened.

She loves children, and is just as playful as other cats, but does have her crazy moments when she races back and forth throughout the house as if the devil were after her. She won't tear apart a toy mouse

TIPS FOR CARE

Because of her weight and size, the Ragdoll needs a lot of space. Instead of a basket, she would much rather roll up on a dog cushion, where she has more room.

Above: Ragdoll bicolor chocolate; the mask must show an upside-down "V."

Center: A white chin and white paws are what make a Ragdoll.

Right: Mitted and color-pointed cats (young animals) have not yet been recognized and are used for breeding.

TYPE AND STANDARD

TYPE, BODY, LEGS, TAIL

A massive cat with a muscular body, a wide, well-developed chest, solid hindquarters, medium-long legs, with the hind legs longer than the front. The female is noticeably smaller than the tom. The tail is long, medium wide at the base, and tapers towards the tip. It is bushy and well covered with hair.

HEAD, EYES, EARS

The medium-sized head is a modified wedge; the nose is slightly bowed at the upper third, and the cheeks are well developed and taper towards the mouth. The ears are of medium size with slightly rounded tips. The eyes are large, oval, and a luminous, intense blue.

COAT

The soft, silken coat is medium long, dense, and close to the body. The coat is longest around the neck and the ruff frames the outline of the face, creating a bib. The coat in the face is short, but somewhat longer starting at the top of the head towards the back and around the shoulders. The hair is medium long to long on the underbelly and the sides, and short to medium long on the hindquarters and the front legs.

COLOR

The Ragdoll comes in three patterns: color pointed, mitted, and bicolored, where the mitted and the color-pointed varieties are not yet recognized but are registered for breeding.

COLOR VARIATIONS

Bicolor: the color on the body should be lighter than the points, white patches on the back are not allowed, the underbelly is white and without patches, the legs should be white, the tip of the nose pink. The points on the ears, mask, and tail must be well defined. The mask must show an upside-down "V." Color: seal, blue, chocolate, lilac.

Mitted: the color on the body and points are the same as the color points, with exception of the paws and chin. The chin should be white, and a white stripe should run towards the nose. The four legs of the mitted cat have white mittens, the hind feet are white up to the heel. A white stripe begins on the bib and runs through the front legs and all the way up to the end of the tail. Color: seal, blue, chocolate, lilac.

Color-pointed: the color of the body must be uniform throughout, lighter than the points. Chest and bib are lighter than the color of the body. The points on the ears, mask, legs, and tail must harmonize with the color of the body. Color: seal, blue, chocolate, lilac.

Above: The eyes should be intense blue.

Below: Bicolor chocolate. The points need to be clearly defined.

as soon as she gets hold of it; curtains won't be used as "climbing posts" just because she was searching for an easier way to reach the top of the shelf. One thing this cat will do is quickly claim a place on your bed, not surprising because she loves and wants to be near people. She is easily trained, will "heel" and retrieve, and come when called. She gets along well with other cats, but because of her stature and size she will be intimidating to animals that are more fragile.

Norwegian Forest

A Surprise from the Cool North

The Norwegian Forest cat might be a natural breed that survived for hundreds of years in close proximity to humans but without direct contact. To this day the Norwegian cat's robustness and adaptability are one of her main characteristics.

ORIGIN

It is possible—even though it cannot be proven—that these robust mouse catchers escaped from the ships of the Vikings: they look typical of house cats of the Middle Ages. However, the rough climate of Scandinavia allowed only the best suited to survive. These cats developed tremendous jumping abilities, a shaggy coat, and a very strong body.

It is likely that these animal also lived for centuries in Siberia without any direct contact with humans. They were discovered at the beginning of the twentieth century in Norway and declared as the country's national cat. As early as the 1930s, fanciers began to breed them intentionally. The breed was recognized in 1977. Because their looks are so different in the summer than in the winter, this new breed was not immediately successful. Not until the middle 1980s did they gain substantial popularity.

Above: A straight profile without a break and a triangularly shaped head.

Left: A furry undercoat is beneath the sleek, water-repellent hair. Bib, full ruff, and knickers as well as a long, bushy tail are the characteristics of the Norwegian Forest.

Left page: The eyes—set on an angle—may be of every available color.

CHARACTER AND TEMPERAMENT

The Norwegian Forest knows how to assert herself; she has energy and an unbelievable ability and desire to adapt. She lives well in a household with many children or with a single person. She cuddles when the owner is affectionate, but will keep to herself when the owner wants to be left alone. She will retain her thin summer coat if she is not allowed to be outside, but will grow a luxurious water-repellent coat when she can experience the changes of the season directly.

She moves with caution and skill on shelves filled with knick-knacks and exercises enthusiastically on her scratching post. She is an intelligent cat, has a sharp mind, and is able to make the best

TIPS FOR CARE

For the Norwegian cat to develop a dense color and knickers during the cold season she needs to have access throughout the year to a balcony or a terrace or the outdoors.

Above right: A great amount of white in the coat is acceptable in all available coat colors, as is the case with this tortie Norwegian.

To the right: Silver tabby —a rare coat color for the Norwegian Forest.

TYPE AND STANDARD

TYPE, BODY, LEGS, TAIL

A large cat with a powerful bone structure, long body, and high legs, with the front legs shorter than those in the back. The tail is long, bushy, and when raised reaches the neck.

HEAD, EARS, EYES

The shape of the head is triangular with a long, straight profile, a strong chin, ears that are wide at the base, with lynx-like tufts on the tips and long tufts inside the ear. The eyes are large, alert, and slightly angled. They show an attentive expression and may have all colors.

COAT

The medium-long coat has a furry undercoat that is covered by a sleek water-repellent top coat. The coat is shiny and covers the back and flanks. A fully developed coat has a bib, a full ruff, and knickers on the hindquarters.

COLOR

All colors are allowed, except chocolate, lilac, cinnamon, and fawn. All colors combined with white are allowed, with the exception of pointed markings.

White is allowed in great patches, as are white flame, a white medallion, or white on the chest, underbelly, and paws.

out of every situation. She gets along well with her cousins and other house pets, including dogs. She is one of the few breeds that won't suffer emotionally when she is taken along on a vacation; and even moving house she considers simply an enrichment of her world.

The most perfect among the Norwegian Forest cats will have a lynx-like ruff and tufts.

Maine Coon

Her Majesty the American

A gentle soul in a powerful body, in need of loving care, yet—something that applies customarily only to dogs—ready to defend like a lion, the Maine Coon is a creature of contradiction ready for any surprise and still predictable.

ORIGIN

Was it—as in the case of the Norwegian Forest cats—a Viking warrior, a Pilgrim, or a French immigrant who brought these cats to North America? Nobody can say for sure. At some point, four to seven hundred years ago, cats were left, perhaps due to shipwrecks, in the almost uninhabited expanses of America, establishing themselves, and successfully living wild. Climate and the food available allowed them to thrive, develop a weather-defying coat and great stamina.

The first part of their name refers to the state of Maine, since it was there that breeders became aware of them for the first time. The second half, "Coon," came compliments of the raccoon because they looked much like them, at least as far as original coat color and look are concerned. This American breed not only became popular with fanciers but won the hearts of all cat lovers to become one of their favorite breeds.

CHARACTER AND TEMPERAMENT

The Maine Coon is wild and tame at the same time: she plays with passion and cuddles with affection, yet she can roam outside for nights on end when she is allowed. She will lay quietly at anybody's feet—or in the lap of her person—without being a bother. She loves company and to go on walks, but will also stay home alone without complaining—if she knows that afterwards she will get a substantial amount of play time.

Above: The wavy coat of the Maine Coon is lighter in the summer; not until the fall will she grow a thick coat.

Left page: The undercoat is fine and covered with a rough, long topcoat.

Right: The large oval eyes should be set far apart and somewhat at an angle; they may be of any color.

Below left: Maine Coon black bicolor; the cat should have a substantial body with a white chest.

Below right: The coat is relatively short on the head, shoulders, and legs, longer at the back and sides, and long, full, and scraggly at the hind legs and the underbelly. The Maine Coon must always have a ruff.

She does so well in the house, in spite of her size, because she wants to please. If something she does causes her people to disapprove, she will try not to do it again, not always successfully—but she will try. If she discovers that one of her pranks makes the person she adores happy, she will repeat it as often as she can. Maine Coon cats greet people when they come home with never-ending enthusiasm just as if they had been away for weeks on end. And good-byes are said with a heart rending sad look as if she thinks she is being left for good. She will comfort people when life is difficult, she will cheer them when they are sad, and she will soothe their frayed nerves. As long as she can dominate she will get along with other cats, as well as dogs and rabbits.

TYPE AND STANDARD

TYPE, BODY, LEGS, TAIL

A large cat with a strong, solid build. The body is long with hard muscles, with a wide chest, and is of square shape. The powerful legs are medium long, have large round paws and tufts between the toes. The tail should be as long as the body, wide at the base, tapering to the tip, with flowing hair.

HEAD, EYES, EARS

The mid-sized head is square and the profile shows a gentle concave indentation; the cheek bones are high and protruding. Between mouth and cheek bones is a distinct transition. The large ears are broad at the base and taper moderately to the tip; they are placed high on the head, leaning slightly to the outside. Inside the ears are lynx-like tufts and bushels of hair that extend beyond the edges. The large, slightly oval-shaped eyes are set wide apart and appear to be round when they are open wide. They are set at a slight angle in the direction of the outer edge of the ears and may come in any color.

COAT

The coat is dense, short on the head, shoulder, and legs and lengthens gradually along the back. The long, full, scraggly hair on the hind legs creates what could be considered harem pants. The coat on the underbelly is also long and scraggly, as is the ruff. The coat is silky, has substance, and flows. The soft, fine under- coat is covered with a more robust smooth topcoat.

COLOR

All colors are allowed, except chocolate, cinnamon, lilac, and fawn. All colors combined with white are allowed.

COLOR VARIATIONS

Black, blue, black and white, blue and white. Black-golden, blue-golden, black-golden with white, blue-golden with white, red-golden, cream-golden, black-tortie golden, blue-tortie golden, red-golden with white, cream-golden with white, black-tortie golden with white, blue-tortie golden with white, black-silver shaded, blue-silver, red-silver, cream-silver, black-tortie silver, blue-tortie silver, black-silver with white, blue-silver with white, red-silver with white, cream-silver with white, black-tortie silver with white, blue-tortie silver with white: all shaded, shell, striped, piebald, spotted, and ticked.

Tabby: black, blue, black with white, blue with white, red, cream, black tortie, blue tortie, red white, cream white, black tortie with white, blue tortie with white: all stripes, piebald, spotted, and ticked.

Smoke: black, blue, red, cream, black tortie, blue tortie, black-silver with white, blue-silver with white, red-silver with white, cream-silver with white, black-tortie silver with white, blue-tortie silver with white.

Eyes can be blue, orange, or odd-eyed.

The ears have Lynx-like brushes and hair tufts.

Persian

A Gentle Beauty
with a Hint of Luxury

Many breeds have—during the course of history—been a part of the development of this magnificent, exotic creature, the epitome of the long-haired cat.

ORIGIN

Whether the Persian cat, which came from Asia to Europe with the merchant seafarers, came from Persia rather than from Turkey remains a mystery. In any case, she is an Asian cat and through mutation has developed a considerably longer coat and a somewhat more stocky build than her house cat sisters. Of course, the original animals by no means had such a luxurious coat as the Persian carries today. But she already carried the gene for long hair—reason enough for the determined breeding enthusiasts in England to refine the quality and length of the coat.

Long before cat-breeding methodology was in vogue and before regular cat exhibitions took place in Europe or the United States, Persian cats were talked about everywhere. They lived at the palaces of kings and were the pampered favorites of artists. More and more colors were created, and they became heavier and rounder until by the mid–1940s the modern Persian cat already had the characteristic snub nose and short face of today's extreme type in the USA. Peke-face (Pekinese-face) was what proud breeders in the United States called this type; however, their creation was not favored or accepted everywhere.

The extreme Persian-cat type has difficulty eating food and also difficulty with breathing. Because the standard does not require a Peke-face, more and more breeders (at least in Europe) are going

Above: Doll-face with a snub nose and a chubby (stocky) body: The Persian.

Below: Chinchilla-Persian: Because of the darker-colored tip of each hair the white cat appears to be darker.

Left page: In the shaded cameo, one third of each hair has a red tip.

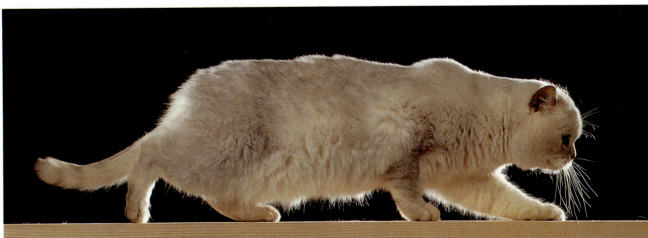

Above: Everything about a Persian is round and impressive: the head with a short nose, small ears which are placed low on the head, the wide chest, and the massive rump.

To the right: In a red-white Persian, a clear distinction between colors is important; they cannot run into one another.

Below right: The coat of the Persian is long, dense, fine and silky, and should not be furry.

She loves to play with a string that is held like a fishing line and will throw herself on her back and try to catch the "prey" with her round paws. She prefers an hour in a lap anytime over an hour's worth of playing games. She loves to cuddle long and intensely without being pushy. She dislikes it if the house is too warm, because with her dense coat she gets hot in the opposite direction, and while they still produce round-faced, snub-nosed Persians, they are healthier and no longer have the extreme short heads. This "backward" development was good for this long-haired feline, who was seen for a time in an unfavorable light and has now again rekindled enthusiasm.

CHARACTER AND TEMPERAMENT

The Persian belongs to the group of cats that are well-mannered and of quiet. Wild runs through the apartment or house are not her style; she would much rather play rolling on the floor. Hunting may be limited to a few moments, but she is just as curious and attentive as her short-haired cousins.

very quickly. Because of her body temperature she is not a "bed" but rather a "sofa" cat. She loves to sit comfortably next to her owner when he is watching TV, and feels secure when the family is gathered around the table and she can look at her loved-ones in peace and contentment. The Persian has a gentle, thin voice, but uses it only rarely.

A solid-colored Persian in blue with copper-colored eyes.

TYPE AND STANDARD

TYPE, BODY, LEGS, TAIL

A large cat with a stocky body, a wide chest, a massive wide back, and short, thick powerful legs with large red paws that have hair tufts between the toes. The tail is short and bushy and slightly rounded at the end.

HEAD, EYES, EARS

The head is round and massive with a rounded forehead, full cheeks, strong chin and wide jaws. The nose is short and has a distinct break. The short ears have rounded tips as well as hair tufts. They are set wide apart and relatively low on the head. The large, round, alert eyes are also set wide apart and are very expressive.

COAT

The coat is long and thick, fine and silky, but not furry—forming an immense ruff around the neck, shoulders, and chest.

RECOGNIZED COLOR VARIATIONS

White with blue, orange, or odd-colored eyes. Solid with copper or dark orange eyes: black, blue, chocolate, lilac, red, cream.

Tortoiseshell with copper or dark orange-colored eyes: black, blue chocolate, lilac.

Smoke with copper or dark orange-colored: black, blue, chocolate, lilac, red, cream, black tortie, blue tortie, chocolate tortie, lilac tortie.

Shaded/shell with green, blue-green, copper or dark orange-colored eyes: black, blue, chocolate, lilac, red, cream, black tortie, blue tortie, chocolate tortie, lilac tortie.

Golden shaded/shell with green or blue-green eyes outlined in black, and black tipping on the tip of the hair.

Tabby (striped, piebald, spotted) with copper or dark orange-colored eyes: black, blue, chocolate, lilac, red, cream, black tortie, blue tortie, chocolate tortie, lilac tortie.

Silver tabby with green, copper or dark orange-colored eyes: black, blue, chocolate, lilac, red, cream, black tortie, blue tortie, chocolate tortie, lilac tortie.

Golden tabby with green or blue green eyes that are outlined in black with black markings.

Two-colored—with white (Van, Harlequin, bicolor)—with deep blue, copper, or dark orange or odd-colored eyes: black, blue, chocolate, lilac, red, cream, black tortie, blue tortie, chocolate tortie, lilac tortie.

Two-colored tabby (striped, piebald, spotted) (Van, Harlequin, bicolor) with deep blue, copper or dark orange or odd-colored eyes: black, blue, chocolate, lilac, red, cream, black tortie, blue tortie, chocolate tortie, lilac tortie.

Himalayan

The Cat with a Mask and a Mane

The Himalayan has the same body type as the Persians, however, the markings are that of a Siamese. In Britain, Himalayans are known as Colorpoint Longhair or Color-point Persian. While according to breeding guidelines she is considered a Persian, this masked cat with the longest hair has a few unique characteristics.

ORIGIN

As early as the mid 1920s, a Swedish geneticist, Dr. Djebbes, was crossing Siamese with Persians. He wanted to know scientifically after how many generations the

long hair and mask marking would appear together. His attempts "created" the first long-haired, masked cat. The scientific study produced a sensation, but the potential for a new breed was not appreciated.

In 1937, American breeders again created long-haired Siamese and called them Himalayan, not because of the mountains in Asia but because of the same masked points found in rabbits and rats that were already described as "Himalayan." This time around, the stocky, masked cat found favor with the public and became recognized in the United States. In Europe, the French followed the American example and produced

Above: Chocolate tabby, with a striped mask.

Left: The markings of the Red-point Himalayan are red.

Left page: Himalayan Seal point: light coat, blue eyes, dark mask and markings.

cats that they called "Khmer," by crossbreeding the same two breeds. But not until fanciers in England started all over again in the 1940s to produce their own "Colorpoint Longhair" was the breed at last successful. The British breeders also gave the breed its Persian-like shape and the still typical mask.

CHARACTER AND TEMPERAMENT

The Himalayan is an all-around lovable cat, kind, always keen for strokes, friendly, demanding, but not pushy, and quiet. She dispenses favors to every member of the family—as long as nobody becomes raucous, because she dislikes roughhousing or hectic activities. She uses her claws on a scratching post or when hunting—very seldom to defend herself. She gets along with other animals as long as they don't come too close.

Above: As far as characteristics are concerned, the Himalayan is similar to standard Persian cats: large and stocky, with long hair. This is a Blue point.

Right: Himalayan Blue point—a modified example where the nose is not quite as short as usual.

Far right: The coat of the Himalayan can grow up to four inches (10 cm) or more.

She will blissfully place herself on a pillow next to her people, contentedly watch when children do their homework, and lovingly greet everyone with a quiet meow when they come home. Every now and then the temperament of the Siamese comes through when the Himalayan races through the house with the hair on her tail standing on end and the ruff around her neck sticking out like porcupine needles. But she will soon be her old self again—quiet and dignified. Persians and Himalayans do well together, but she will get along with other breeds only if she is able to stay out of their way.

TYPE AND STANDARD

Himalayan—according to TICA standard—is considered a Persian cat, and her build and coat reflect that. The only exception: the eyes must always be blue.

RECOGNIZED COLOR VARIATIONS

All color variations have the pointed Himalyan patternimg.
Solid point: Seal, blue, chocolate, lilac, red, cream.
Tortie point: seal, blue, chocolate, lilac.
Tabby point (lynx point): seal, blue, chocolate, lilac, red, cream.
Torbie point (tortie lynx point): seal, blue, chocolate, lilac.

Himalayan Blue point: the hair at the tail is particularly dense and long.

NOTE

Lynx Point is the combination of Tabby markings with Himalayan patterning. Similarly, Torbie Point can be described as Tortie Lynx Point.

TIPS FOR CARE

The coat on the hindquarters becomes matted easily if dirt is not brushed out completely. As is the case with Persian cats, set aside half an hour daily for grooming.

Exotic Shorthair

Chubby Cheeks
with a Cuddly Coat

The Exotic Shorthair has all the lovable characteristics of the Persian but without the high-maintenance coat. This gentle, people-oriented, cuddly cat with a baby face captivates with her snuggly body and dense, furry coat.

ORIGIN

Breeders in America have long bred Persian cats with their domestic cats to try to create a typical "American Shorthair" type of Persian. But these short-haired, snuggly cats were considered "illegal" because they did not have a proper pedigree. Still that did not keep people from falling in love with them. They sold tremendously well and in 1967 the CFA recognized this short-legged kitten with the furry coat as the Exotic Shorthair. The name "Exotic" was

Above left: A truly cuddly cat—chubby, standing on stout legs, and with a baby face.

Left: Exotic Shorthair Chinchilla: the eyes, because of the dark make-up, are particularly impressive.

Above right: With her large, round, alert eyes, the Exotic Shorthair always has an expression of slight amazement.

Left page: A dense furry coat, standing slightly away from the body, characterizes the Exotic Shorthair.

chosen to link these cats to the Persian but distinguish them from the American Shorthair. The cat did not have it quite as easy in Eu-

Above: When light falls on the coat of the Exotic Shorthair, it becomes obvious that it is not nearly as "short" as other short-haired breeds.

To the right: The characteristic M-shape on the forehead can also be seen on the tabby Exotic Shorthair.

rope—after all, the British Shorthair also had a stout build and that typical baby face, with chubby cheeks as well as a snub nose. It took until 1984 for TICA to recognize this "Shorthair Persian" and assign her a separate standard.

CHARACTER AND TEMPERAMENT

This baby-faced cat with an expression that seems to signal slight amazement is not all that innocent, and, while she is rather quiet and loves comfort, she is capable of getting herself all worked up. However, such scenes are the exception. Generally speaking, the Exotic Shorthair is almost unbelievably friendly—genuine towards all.

TYPE AND STANDARD

TYPE, BODY, LEGS, TAIL

A large, stocky cat with a wide chest, massive shoulders, and a well-muscled back. Short, thick, strong legs with large, round, firm paws. The tail is short, well covered with hair, and slightly rounded at the tip.

HEAD, EYES, EARS

The massive head has a rounded forehead, well-developed cheeks, and a short, wide nose with a definite stop. The chin is prominent. The small ears are slightly rounded at the tip. The large, round eyes are set wide apart and are very expressive.

COAT

The coat is dense, plush, and soft, and stands slightly upright. It is somewhat longer than that of the British Shorthair but not long enough for the hair to appear to be flowing.

RECOGNIZED COLOR VARIATIONS

All colors of the Persian, Colorpoint, and American Shorthairs are recognized.

Her fondness for snuggling is very developed. She does not care to go outdoors but would rather sit for hours in one place and philosophize; she can stare with large, round eyes at a leaf or a knick-knack with only a slight twitching of the ears to indicate that she is not a stuffed cat. She will reward with loud purring those who consistently give her the hugs and strokes she desires. She will then contentedly roll over, expecting some tummy rubs. She hates to be ignored and can pout for hours, which she knows will eventually bring her the attention she feels she deserves. Since almost nobody can resist her enduring charm, she always succeeds in getting the best tidbits—and usually exactly when she wants them.

Above: Short legs are supported by large, round, powerful paws.

Above left: Blue Cream Exotic Shorthair: each individual hair has a different color.

TIPS FOR CARE

Because of the dense undercoat and the dense cover hair, the Exotic Shorthair should be thoroughly brushed once a week to stimulate circulation in the skin.

Index